EXTENSION AND COMMUNICATION MANAGEMENT

SATWIK BISARYA | SAVITA SINGH

Made with ♥ on the Notion Press Platform
www.notionpress.com

This book is dedicated to my late father who taught me to be an independent and determined person, to my doting mother without whom I would never be able to achieve my objectives and succeed in life, and to all my diligent students whose feedback has always helped me to be a better teacher.

- Dr. Satwik Sahay Bisarya

Contents

Author's Affiliation

Dr. Satwik Sahay Bisarya, Dean and Associate Professor, Faculty of Agriculture Science and Technology, Madhyanchal Professional University, Bhadbhada Road, Ratibad, Madhya Pradesh - 462044

Ms. Savita Singh, Research Scholar, Faculty of Commerce & Management, Madhyanchal Professional University, Bhadbhada Road, Ratibad, Madhya Pradesh - 462044

Preface

The book planned under the programme with a strong foundation for the two aspects of Extension and Communication. The issues of national concern are reflected in the curriculum with a focus on linking women and children to mainstream national development programmes. It will orient the students to the socio-cultural and economic environment of rural, urban and semi urban communities. The course will prepare a cadre of professionals to work with governmental and non-governmental organisations in various capacities. It will enhance self-employment potential through entrepreneurial skill training by developing competency in the preparation of participatory and innovative communication strategies for the dissemination of vital information to vulnerable sections of the population. The course gives an insight how to channelise the potential to become development Media specialists with an orientation to Development Journalism, Media Research and sensitivity to the vast heritages and oral traditions of the country. It also helps to develop skills in planning, implementing, monitoring and evaluating various programmes in the developmental sector.

CHAPTER I

COMMUNICATION PROCESS IN DEVELOPMENT

The word communication originates from the Latin word 'Communis' which means common. That means we share common thoughts, feelings and ideas with the person with whom we are communicating with a commonness of understanding. We make use of speech, writing, printed and pictorial matter, gestures and expressions also of technical media like telegraphy, radio, television, computer etc. for communication.

Usually, Communication is a continuous process of giving and receiving information and building up social relationships. So, concisely communication is "a process by which two or more people exchange ideas, facts, feelings or impressions in ways that which gains a common understanding of the message."

Let us see what are the characteristics of communication:

i. ***Communication is a two way process***: It involves a sender and receiver. Who can be an individual or a group.
ii. **There can also be message:** This deals with the information or a directive or an enquiry, a feeling, an opinion, an idea or any other instruction also.
iii. ***Commonness of understanding***: Communication can occur only when there is commonness of understanding between the sender and the receiver. This includes the factors like common culture, common language, common environment, words, phrases, idioms, proverbs, gestures, expressions are deeply cultured and also possess high communicative potential for people from similar background.
iv. ***Modifying the behavior of other individuals***: This is the main purpose of the communication where the information

transmitted to the receiver receives a response in the form of some change in the behaviour of the individual.

v. ***Method of giving information***: The information can be given through words or through other means like signs, gestures and expressions etc.

The importance of communication has been widely recognized in recent years. And the need for effective communication becomes clear when you go through the following statements

- Human existence is impossible without communication.
- Information is every individual's need. Through communication information need is satisfied.
- Individuals make decisions every minute and communication helps in decision- making.
- Whether family or any other institution for that matter, cannot function without communication. And this can be achieved through coordination and cooperation.
- Education aims at behavioral change. Intended behavioral change can be achieved only through the communication.
- Disputes and conflicts are settled through negotiations, that is also one form of communication through which the peace and harmony is established.
- Individuals vary in capacities and efficiencies where the communication demonstrates individual efficiencies.
- Also individuals vary in their performances through effectively evaluating the individual performance and
- Every second many changes occur in the world. They keep people informing about those changes.
- Leadership action, which is impossible without communication between the leader and his followers that is main basic for the leadership action.
- Whether teacher or student, lawyer or client, marketer or consumer, whether it is farmer or extension worker or wherever it is the work goes on, job satisfaction is very much essential that

provides through the communication process.

Regarding the Purpose of communication, first and foremost things the organizations are large in number and the people working in the organization to achieve a common goal are employed for the sake of showing the organizational hierarchy through communication. This leads to the coordination and also synchronizing all the activities of various groups or departments of the organizations.

Finally, it leads the ***Smooth Working of the*** enterprise or the organization to a greater extent, where you can have a very good communication network.

Effective decision-making also is one of important aspect, which will be contributing towards the organizational success through communication. Whether it is past or present they are being provided for quick and effective decision-making. All the figures will be communicated by the organization to the people working there. An effective communication network which supplies information helps in arriving at quick decisions. Problem-defining, alternative courses of action selecting the best course of action are all possible only with necessary information supplied to the decision- maker.

Managerial Efficiency: This is also one of the important component of Communication process which will be contributing for the success of an organization. Management is an art of getting things done through other people; it is communication that will be educating people working in the organization about the goals, policies and targets by issuing orders and instructions orally as well as in written form. Therefore, managerial efficiency lies in the way the manager communicates with the individual or group in an organization.

Co-operation: Co-operation among workers, are possible with the exchange of information between individuals and groups and between the management and the employee's co-operation promotes industrial peace and maximum production.

A leader leads his followers through a continuous process of communication. Communication is the basis for directing, and motivating the follower and the followers in turn follow him by conveying ideas, opinions, feelings, and facts.

Openness and frank expression of opinions from both sides lead to job satisfaction.

It is through communication that the workers can be well informed about the process of production, new methods of production, the activities of the workers in a similar organization. So, a good system of communication helps in management to achieve maximum productivity with minimum cost, and by elimination of waste.

Morale Building: When clear instructions are given to the employees it is easy to achieve the goals of the organization. In turn, the management needs to appreciate the works of the employees. An effective system of communication builds good morale and improves human relationships and also encourage the employees. Participatory communication is the best technique of morale building and motivation also.

A manager normally performs three roles. i.e. inter-personal roles, informational roles and decision roles. Communication plays a vital role in all these three types of roles. In the case of inter-personal role a manager has to interact with the subordinates. In the information role, he has to collect information from various people and supply it to others both inside and outside the organization. A Manager in a decisional role takes important decisions based on the interpersonal and informational communication.

CHAPTER II

ELEMENTS AND PROCESS OF COMMUNICATION

Elements and Process of communication: The Communication can be expected to have taken place only if the message is encoded by the sender that is relayed with use of signals and subsequently decoded at the destination. This process occurs, basically due to the presence of five important elements of communication.

Five Basic elements of communication are:

- Source
- Receiver
- Channel
- Message and
- Feedback

Coming to the first element of communication

Source: This is the originator of message who is an individual of formal or informal institution and he is the person who is initiating the message.

Message: This deals with the package of information or the content to be transferred to the receiver. Message deals with the package of information or content to be transferred by the source. In fact, message is the physical product from the source that supply information, create feelings and impressions and change attitudes of the receivers.

Channel: This is the carrier of the message. It may be natural that involves one of the sense modalities like seeing, hearing, touching, smelling, tasting or it may be artificial such as newspaper, radio, television, telephone etc.

Receiver: He is the final consumer of the message in the communication process. All the factors, which determine the success of the source in communication process, are also applicable to. The receiver, i.e., communication skills, attitudes, knowledge level and socio-cultural context.

The last element is Feedback: without feedback, any Communication is never complete. Feedback means carrying some significant responses of the audience back to the communicator. Adequate and correct feedback is essential for purposeful communication. It also provides an opportunity to take corrective measures by identifying subsequent activities, and acts as a pathfinder for enhancing communication effectiveness.

Ways of communication:

The first and foremost way of communication is One-way:

The one-way communication is transferred in only one direction, i.e. from the sender to the receiver. There isn't any opportunity for the receiver to give the feedback to the sender.

Next type of communication will be Two way communication : This is a form of transmission in which both parties are involved in transmitting the information. Two-Way communication has also been referred to as interpersonal communication.

Common forms of two-way communication, I can just give you some examples like

- Amateur Radio, or different types of FM radios where for short range you have radio contacts and through the devices like walkie-talkies, other instruments the information can be interchanged or transmitted.
- Chartrooms, Instant Messaging, Computer networks, In-person communication, that is related to business within the organization.

All this is nothing but, two-way communication. Here you can just resolve the problems more efficiently, fastly, quickly and generating long-term relationships are possible by resolving problems and setting everything right. Telephone also a good example for this two-way communication, that can be between neighbours or friends or even the business.

The last way of communication is Interactive communication: As noted earlier, communication is a dynamic interactive process. It consists of five steps, that is ideation, encoding, transmission, decoding, and response.

The first step Ideation is the formation of the idea or selection of a message to be communicated. It consists of the "what" of communication and is concerned with the content of the specific message to be presented.

The second step in communication process is Encoding: It is the main process where the information is being changed into some form of logical and coded message. It is based on the purpose of communication and also the relation between the sender and the receiver. It involves:

1. Selecting a language
2. Selecting a medium of communication; and also
3. Selecting an appropriate communication

Next aspect in the process is Transmission: This refers to the flow of message over the chosen channel. It confirms the medium selected during the process of encoding and keeps the communication channel free from interference or noise so that the message reaches the receiver without any disturbance. It is one of the most basic aspects of communication because it also involves choosing the proper time (when to communicate) or proper place (where to communicate), and a proper way (how to communicate).

Next aspect in the process is Decoding: This is the process of converting the message into thoughts by translating the received stimuli in to an interpreted meaning in order to understand the message communicated. It is important to note that it is the message that is transferred, as meaning cannot be transferred from one person to another. The receiver has to assign meaning to a message in order to understand it.

The last important element is Response: The Response is the last stage in the communication process. It is the action or reaction of the receiver to the message. It helps the sender know that the message was received and understood. The feedback that goes to the sender makes it clear whatever the receiver has accepted the information and field it in his/her memory or rejected it. He or she may ask for more information or clarifications also. Response is, thus, the key to communication as the effectiveness of communication depends upon how congruent a receiver's response is with the meaning intended by the sender.

CHAPTER III

EXISTING PATTERNS OF COMMUNICATION

The first one is Intrapersonal communication: Communication that takes place within oneself is intra personal communication. No other person will be involved here and there is no provision of feedback or also it is just an internal process.

- interpreting maps, texts, signs, and symbols
- Communication between body parts; saying that, "My stomach is telling me it's time for lunch."
- Day-and night dreaming All these are examples.

Interpersonal communication: This is basically communication between two or more people and it is very informal, such as when you talk to a friend during lunch break, or when you just communicate to your teacher regarding registering about a course, all these things.

The common functions in interpersonal communication are nothing but just listening, talking and discussing.

The third one Group communication: This communication occurs among three or more members and it is based on number of individuals and it can be classified into two types, small group and large group.

In the Small Group Communication, it will be at least between three members of group and also at the maximum around twelve to fifteen members. Example for this type of communication is, a professional group, an educational group or a social group communication. Here they will be having a common bond and a interest and a goal also. A family of three talking at dinner table, all these are very good examples for small group communication.

Large group communication refers to communication in big organizations having a large numbers of individuals including communities brought together by need or self- identification. They can be people of a particular geographical area as the people of the village or town. People who have gathered in hundreds to attend conventions, seminars or conferences can also be very good examples for large group communication.

Any organization, there will be two types of communication, i.e. basically formal or Informal communication.

Formal communication takes place along the lines of authority and this will be established by the management. There are clear guidelines on who should communicate with whom and how to communicate the information. So the policy manuals, rules and procedures, reports & books, memoranda, official meetings all these comes under the formal type of communication.

Formal type of communication has many advantages: It helps in the fixation of responsibility, maintaining the authority relationships.

Disadvantages are generally with procedures to be followed many times, the misunderstanding or distortions occurs regarding the following of rules and regulations.

Another type is Informal communication. This is usually built around the social relationships among members of the society. There will not be any rules and regulations and they are almost like channels of communication arises due to the personal needs only.

This is really difficult to fix responsibility and part of the accuracy of information, so the information can also become the rumours and usually it is oral in nature and with just a simple glance, gesture or smile or silence also sometimes becomes informal communication and it is not possible to identify the source of communication also. We can we say there the communication ends also.

Another one is Mass communication: this is the term used to relay information to large segments of the population at the same time. And it refers to newspaper & magazine publishing, radio, television, films etc., it is also used for disseminating news and giving some advertisements also.

Factors that help or hinder communication: All the communication should try to persuade and not rush or overwhelm the people. There will be lots of barriers and those should be overcome through persuasion only. Proper arrangement also should

be made to obtain the feedback and sooner you get the feedback the sooner you will be able to change your mode and improve the communication manner and then only the communication will be effective.

Always the **sender should make sure,** to whom should the message go? Why am I communicating? What are my motives? Decide what to communicate. Be clear about what you need to communicate. Choose the best time for optimum reception. Use language the receiver can understand and which is unambiguous. Choose a location, which will not interfere with the reception, understanding and acceptance of the message. Keep checking with the receiver.

Receiver always should be fully ATTENTIVE, Listen ACTIVELY, ASK for clarifications, reception where necessary. Keep checking with sender.

So, to facilitate Communication:

1. **We should have a positive attitude about the communication**: Defensiveness interferes with the communication.
2. **Work at improving communication skills**: It also takes knowledge and work. The communication model and discussion of barriers to communication provide the necessary knowledge. This increased awareness of the potential for improving communication is the first step to better communication.
3. **One should Make communication goal oriented**: Relational goals come first and pave way for other ones. When the sender or the receiver have a good relationship, they are much more likely to accomplish their communication goals.

4. **Approach communication as a creative process** rather than simply part of the chore of working with people will become almost like a lack of communication and meaningless communication. Vary channels, listening techniques, and feedback techniques are also very important.
5. **Accept the reality of miscommunication**: The best communicators fail to have perfect communication. They accept miscommunication and work to minimize its negative impacts.

The barriers of communication, there are many types of barriers of communication:

First and foremost Physical Barriers: Emotional disturbances like traffic noise, loud sound, passing train, Time and Distance Personal Problems, health also comes in way, Poor hearing due to defective hearing, Poor presentation due to speech defects like stammering, lisping etc. Poor verbal skills also comes under the Physical Barriers.

Noisy transmission, unreliable messages, inconsistency, difference in the communication very often becomes the barrier like non-availability of proper machines or presence of defective machines and wrong channels or medium also becomes the **Mechanical Barriers.**

Coming to the Mental Barriers: From the sender's point of view ignorance of the language and confused thinking are the mental barriers.

From the receiver's point of view ignorance of the language, Limitations inability, intelligence and understanding divided attention are the serious **mental barriers.**

The Semantic Problems occur when people use either the same word in different ways or different words in the same way. The choice of words or language in which a sender encodes a message will influence the quality of communication.

Receiver distortion: This is selective hearing, ignoring non-verbal cues, **Voice control** - Pitch, modulation of voice helping in making communication effective. This is very important in the field of communication and this should be thought properly by the Communicators also.

Coming to the Cross Cultural Barriers – Effective communication requires simply converting the basic values, motives, aspirations, and assumptions that operate across geographical lines.

Socio-psychological barriers are Values, Attitudes and Opinions.

Pre-conceived notions: We judge people before they speak by allowing our opinions and ideas of them come in the way of trying to know what the speaker is saying.

Assumptions: Like seeing others situation same as yours, has the same feelings as you comes under this socio-psychological barriers.

Status effects like power struggles

Defensiveness: distorted perceptions, guilt, projection, transference, distortions from the past, negative emotions, distrusted source, erroneous translation, value judgment, state of mind of two people comes under the same type of barriers.

Interpersonal Relationships are also some type of barriers which effect the communication in perception by the past experience with the individual or also affected by the organizational relationship between two people. We show through an example, from a superior, he may be perceiving differently than that of the side of a subordinate or peer.

CHAPTER IV

CLASSIFICATION OF METHODS IN DEVELOPMENT COMMUNICATION

A method, this is a procedure or process for attaining an objective. The choice of a channel or method of communication is also known as extension method, generally depends on the number and location of the target audience and the time available for communication. They are categorized as individual method, group method and mass method. The extension methods are the tools and techniques used to create situations in which communication can takes place between the rural people and the extension workers. They are the methods of extending new knowledge & skills to the rural people by drawing their attention towards them, arousing their interest & helping them to have a successful experience of the new practice.

A proper understanding of these methods & their selection for a particular type of work are necessary.

Classification of Methods in development communication:

One way of classifying the extension methods is according to their use & nature of contact. In other words, they are used for contacting people individually, or in groups or in masses.

Based upon the nature of contact, they are divided into individual method, group method & mass method as I told you earlier.

Under the individual contact methods there are methods like Farm and home visit, Farmer's call, Personal letter, Adaptive or minikit trail, Farm clinic and Result demonstration.

Under the group methods there are method demonstration, group meeting, small group training, field day or farmer's day and study tour.

And under the mass contact methods we have farm publication, mass meetings, campaigns, exhibitions, newspapers and also radio and television methods which can be usually employed for the sake of contacting the farmers or as well as the rural women.

Under the **Individual-contact methods** we can understand that they are to provide opportunities for face- to-face and personal contact or person-to-person contact between the rural people & the extension workers. These methods are very effective in teaching new skills & creating goodwill between farmers & the extension workers.

The Group-contact methods: the rural people or farmers are contacted in group which usually consists of 20 to 25 persons. These groups are usually formed around the common interest. These methods also involve a face-to-face contact with the people & provide an opportunity for exchange of ideas, for discussions on problems & technical recommendations & finally for deciding the future course of action.

Mass or community-contact methods are mainly employed by the extension worker so as to approach the people or the public in the larger number of masses for disseminating new information & helping them to use it conveniently. These methods are more useful for making people aware of the new technologies quickly.

Individual methods - applicability, advantages and disadvantages

So in this method, the extension agent communicates with the people individually, maintaining separate identity of each person.

The method of applicability is followed when the numbers of people will be contacted and they will be few in number, conveniently located close to the communicator and there will be sufficient time available for communication. I have already given the examples such as Farm and home visit, farmers call Personal letters, Farmer's call / office call, Farm clinic Adaptive or Minikit trial methods etc.

Under the **Farm and Home Visit,** it is a direct, face –to – face contact by the extension agent with the farmer or homemaker at the farm or even sometimes at home for the sake of the extension work that need to be carried out.

The **Farmer's call** is a call made by the farmer or homemaker at the working place of the extension agent for obtaining information and assistance.

The **Personal letter** is written by the extension agent to particular farmer or homemaker in connection with the extension work. This should not be regarded as a substitute for personal contact.

And the **Farmer's clinic** is a facility developed and extended to the farmers for diagnosis and treatment of farm problems and to provide some specialist advice to individual farmers

There is also **Adaptive or minikit trail method,** which is for the determining the suitability or otherwise of a new practice in farmer's situation

The Advantages of all these individual contact methods are:

- To help the extension agent in building rapport
- Facilitate gaining firsthand knowledge of farm and home
- Helping in selection of demonstrators and local leaders
- Helps in changing attitude of the people
- Helps in teaching complex practices
- Facilitates transfer of technologies
- Enhances effectiveness of group and mass contacts
- Facilitates getting feedback information

But there are some limitations , such as

- This method is time consuming and relatively expensive also
- Has low coverage of audience
- And the extension agent may develop favoritism or bias towards some persons only

Group methods - applicability, advantages and disadvantages

Coming to the group contact methods in detail, it is contacting as an aggregate of a small number of people in reciprocal communication and interaction around some common interest. In this method, the extension agent communicates with the people in groups and not as individual persons.

Regarding the applicability of this method, it is adopted when it is necessary to communicate with a number of people simultaneously, who are located not far off from the communicator.

And the examples are Method and Result demonstration, General meetings, group meetings, Group discussions with Lectures, Panels, Symposium, Group interviews, Forum, Debate, Workshop, Seminar, Conference, Buzz sessions, Brain storming, small group trainings like Field Days or Farmer Days, Study Tours and Field trips.

The Demonstrations are the oldest, best, and simplest tools for transmitting sophisticated technology in a simple and understandable form Small group training is a technique of imparting specific skills to a group of people who need them by creating an appropriate learning situation. And the Demonstrations may be of two types.

1. Method demonstrations
2. **Result demonstrations**

Method demonstration is essentially skill training given for a group of people to show how to carry out an entirely new practice or an old practice in a better way.

And the...

Result demonstration is a method of motivating the people for adoption of a new practice by showing it distinctly superior result.

And the General meetings, they include all kinds of meetings held by extension workers. And among these, there are Group meetings which are method of democratically arriving at a certain decisions by a group of people, by taking into consideration the member's points of view. They can also called discussion meetings such as lecture forums, discussion forums, panel discussions, Symposiums, Group interviews, Forum dialogue or public conversation, Debate discussion and Workshops.

Lecture method is giving lecture on various aspects of the subject in which he wants the students to learn.

Panel discussion is an informal conversation put on for the benefits of the audience, by a small group of people 2- 8 in number.

Symposium is a short series of lectures usually by two or five speakers each with different viewpoints. Audience are encouraged addressing questions and comments.

A Group interview where the leader interviews persons on a platform followed by Leader-dominated panel discussion and excellent way for getting information from the experts.

Forum dialogue is usually two volunteers selected from audience discuss a question on which they may or may not have opposite views followed by discussion.

In Debate discussion also teams of usually two or three persons discuss controversial subjects and each speaker speaks for the allotted time.

In Workshop a special type of working conference of a week or of more duration. There are lectures, individual conferences, and emphasis on working groups. Work sessions are also arranged under the guidance of consultants.

Seminars are short term training programmes arranged for a few days-a day or two maximum three days. Seminars are convened to have in depth discussion on a subject from the view of various view points.

And Conference is where all the members are expected to have more or less equal knowledge. It varies between two to three days, maximum of five days. It is a methodology suited to executives and senior officers in dealing with the complex problem which requires the contribution from senior officers to solve the same problem.

There are also **Buzz sessions** which is with large group when there is limited time for discussion, the audience may be divided into smaller units for a short period.

There is also **Brain Storming,** which is a type of small group interaction designed to encourage the free introduction of ideas on an unrestricted basis and without any limitations to feasibility. Participants are encouraged to list for a period of time all the ideas that come to their minds regarding some problems and are asked not to judge the outcome.

Small group training is a technique of imparting specific skills to a group of people who need them by creating an appropriate learning situation.

Field days or Farmer's day, which is also a method of motivating the people to adopt a new practice by showing what has actually been achieved by applying the practice under field conditions

There are also **Study Tours,** which is a visit of group of interested persons accompanied and guided by one or more extension agents out of their neighborhood to study and learn significant improvements in farm and home elsewhere.

There are also **Field trips,** which are excellent means of providing opportunities to participants to observe and experience things/ objects/activities in natural settings. When the participants are exposed to real world, they get firsthand experience and can relate their practical experience with theory.

Regarding the Advantages of group contact methods...

- They enable the extension agent to have face- to-face contact with a number of people at a time
- They Can reach a select part of the target group
- Facilitates sharing of knowledge and experience and thereby strengthen learning of the group members
- They reach fewer people, but offer more opportunities for interaction and feedback
- They also satisfies the basic urge of people for social contacts
- Motivate people to accept change due to group influence
- They are more effective than mass method in stimulating action

- They are less expensive than individual method due to more coverage

Coming to the Limitations:

- Wide diversity in the interest of group members which may create a difficult learning situation
- Holding a meeting may be regarded as an objective in itself

- There can be vested interests, caste groups and village factions which hinder free interaction and decision making by the group members also in this method.

Mass methods - applicability, advantages and disadvantages

The next method is Mass contact method. In this method, the extension agent communicates with a vast and heterogeneous mass of people, without taking into consideration of their individual and group identity.

And the method applicability is adopted where a large and widely dispersed audience is to be communicated within a short time.

For example there are Campaigns, Exhibitions, Mass meetings, Newspapers through which the public will be contacted and also through Radio and Television

A campaign is an intense educational activity for motivating and mobilizing a community to action, to solve a problem or satisfy a need urgently felt by it. A campaign may be for a single day on a theme like Water for life, for a few weeks as in family planning, for a few months as in Vanamahotsava campaign and for a few years as in 'Grow More Food' campaign.

And another type is **Exhibition. This** is a systematic display of models, specimens, charts, photographs, pictures, posters, information etc. in a sequence around a theme to create awareness and interest in the community. Though an exhibition is organized around a major theme, other related themes and some unrelated themes like entertainment may also be included to make the people get attracted towards the exhibition. Farmer's fairs or kisan melas held in which field visit, training programmes are also combined with exhibition and that becomes more effective and popular.

The **Mass meetings** are held to communicate interesting and useful information to a large audience at the same time. And the size of the audience for mass meeting may be a few hundreds, but at the time of fairs or festivals it may be few thousands also.

And the **Dramatization aspect. Dramatization** is a substitute for the real experience in the mass contact methods and the essential process of communication, in which both participant and the spectator are engaged.

Drama is a theatrical performance around the theme by some people who have rehearsed for it. There are many types of dramatized experiences such as plays through radio and television, pageants a type of community drama, usually based on local history, presented by local actors, and produced out of doors, Talking doll restricted to the availability of an expert ventriloquist, who not only project his own voice, but is also able to manipulate the movement of the doll to synchronize with the voice, there is also Puppetry like shadow, rod, finger, stick, glove puppets and marionettes and Psychodrama, Socio-drama, Role-playing are the best examples for this dramatizing aspect.

Coming to the Advantages of Mass contact methods:

- They are very much suitable for creating general awareness among the people
- And it helps in transferring knowledge and forming and changing opinions
- Large number of people may be communicated within a short time
- Facilitates quick communication in times of emergency
- So it reinforces previous learning
- And also naturally less expensive because of more coverage

Coming to the Limitations of Mass contact methods:

- It is less intensive method
- There is little scope for personal contact with the audience
- And there is also little opportunity for interaction with the audience and among the audience
- Generalized recommendations hinder application by the individuals
- And there is little control over the response of the audience also
- There is also lots of difficulty in getting the feedback of information and evaluation of results because there will not be any direct audience in this method.

Selection and use of methods in development communication

Coming to the aspect of selection and use of methods in development communication there is no rule-of-a thumb cannot be given for the selection and use of these various extension methods to ensure success in all situations. However, some guiding principles will be helpful in general. And we must reach more people, teach them more often and keep down the cost of the contact. In order to get most effective results, the extension worker should

1. Select the appropriate methods
2. Have a suitable combination of the selected methods
3. Use them in a proper sequence, so as to have repetition in a variety of ways

Regarding the audience we have to think some factors keeping in our mind in selection of the methods.

The first and foremost is...

a. **Individual and collective differences of the people whom you contact:** The People vary greatly in their

- Knowledge, Attitude, Skills
- Position in Diffusion and adoption
- Educational training, their age, income level, social status, religious beliefs etc.

Some are ''eye-minded'' while other are ''ear – minded'' also. These individual and collective differences influence the teaching approach also. So, people with little or no education and low income may respond to personal visits and result demonstration techniques. People with better education may respond to group meetings and discussion, exhibitions and written materials.

b. **Coming to the Size of Audience:**

- Group Discussion cannot be used effectively for more than 30 participants
- Method Demonstration can be used for relatively small audience
- Lecture can be used for larger audience.

So we need to also remember and keep in mind regarding the teaching objective selection also.

- Nature of change aimed at – is it thinking, attitude or action. That is to be taken care of.
- And you can also take into consideration how to Arrive at a consensus of opinion and arrange a Group Discussion also. And through that you can just come to one consensus regarding one objective and you can then proceed.

Regarding The Subject matter

- If a new practice is simple or familiar than news article, radio are most effective
- For complex practices face to face contacts, written materials and Audio visual aids are more effective

Regarding the Stage of Development of Extension Organization: This is still in initial stage in the country and also if organization is in initial stages of extension, result demonstration is necessary to gain Confidence

Size of Extension Staff also plays a greater role in selection and use of these methods. It is in relation to the Extension clientele - the larger the number of the extension Workers, the greater the scope for direct or personal contact method.

The Availability of Certain Communication media like News papers, Telephone, radio also will be affected for the selection of the type of methods.

And also the amount to be spended upon these methods also affect the type of method.

An extension worker's familiarity also plays a great role and he may be in a position to influence the choice and use of methods also. And that also will be very much playing role in the selection of these methods.

But usually any extension worker, he tries to employ these methods with a combination of methods.

- Like for example as the number of methods of exposure to the extension information increases, the number of farm families changing the behavior increases.
- When it is coming to the percentages of imparting the information or change in the people Seeing and doing plays an important role. But it gives only 6.67% up to the information.
- Seeing, doing and hearing together gives 37.49%
- Seeing, doing, hearing, with reinforcement of reading– 49.29%
- Seeing, doing, hearing, reinforced by reading, personal contacts it stands until 69.99%
- Seeing, doing, hearing, reinforced by reading, personal contacts, more hearing and again seeing it gives up to 78.69%
- And lastly Seeing, doing, hearing, reinforced by reading and also personal contacts, more hearing, seeing and some amount of indirect influence also gives up to 100% change in the behavior

of the individuals.

SO USING THESE METHODS IN PROPER SEQUENCE ALWAYS INCLUDES THE METHODS THAT

- Enable our farmers to see, hear and do the things to be learned
- Enable to reach large number of people and
- Create confidence in themselves.

In order to get most effective results, the extension worker should select the appropriate methods, have a suitable combination of the selected methods, use them in a proper sequence, so as to have repetition in a variety of ways. A proper understanding of these methods & their selection for a particular type of work are always necessary for efficiently communicating to the rural masses to bring change in the knowledge, attitudes and behavior of the people.

CHAPTER V

MEDIA AND DEVELOPMENT COMMUNICATION

Media is a powerful instrument in integrating diversified society like India. It can create an ethos of change and progress. Media is defined as forms, means or channels through which identical information is transmitted to a large number of people at different places.

Media is very important for development planners, practitioners, industrialists, business people, scientists, farmers and even every layman. Through media only economic, social, educational and technological awareness can be created with lesser time. After developmental transformation in India, media became development supportive, flexible, need based especially in rural areas, in the areas of health, nutrition, family welfare, agriculture and dairy development etc.

Different types of media help in stimulating the sensory organs like ears and eyes and facilitate quick comprehension of the message by the audience. These may be used for literate as well as for illiterate people. The technological media or learning devices are added devices that help the instructor to clarify, establish, co-relate and co-ordinate accurate concepts, interpretations and appreciations and enable to make learning more concrete, effective, interesting, inspirational, meaningful and vivid. The audio visual aids are the stimuli for learning 'why', 'how', 'when' and 'where'. The hard to understand principles are usually made clear by the intelligent use of skillfully designed audio-visual media.

Coming to the Classification of audio visual media: Broadly, audio-visual media are classified into Print media, Folk media and Electronic media.

Audio visual Media are instructional devices through which the message can be heard and seen simultaneously. They are used as strategy for communicating the message based on the type of message to be conveyed to the audience.

Print media is one of the most flourishing sectors of the country, which involves various publications through written communication like newspapers, bulletins, magazines, books, folders, pamphlets and journals etc.

Coming to the different types of printing materials, we can have newspaper, which is a publication containing news and advertising, usually printed on low-cost paper like newsprint.

Another one is Tabloids: Half the size of the usual size of newspaper/ broadsheets at 380 mm by 300 mm, and often perceived as sensationalist in contrast to broadsheets.

Magazine: A magazine is a periodical publication containing a variety of articles, generally financed by advertising or purchase by readers.

There are also Journals, which are collection of articles usually written by scholars in an academic or professional field. An editorial board reviews these articles to decide whether they can be accepted or not.

There are also Books, which are collection of sheets of paper, parchment or other material with a piece of text written on them, bound together along one edge within covers. A book is also a literary work or a main division of such work.

There are also Booklets, which are small book or group of pages.

E-books, which are in electronic format.

Leaflets: A single sheet of paper used for presentation of information on one topic in a concise way and in simple language and also they are also called flyers.

There are also Pamphlets, this is also a single printed page used for advertising an event, service or other activity.

Handouts: Handout is something given freely. It can refer to materials handed out for presentation purposes or to a charity gift, among other things. This may refer to short, usually single page assignments distributed in high school or college.

News Letter: A newsletter is a regularly distributed publication generally about one topic of interest to its subscribers. A newsletter deals with current items of interest and is printed periodically.

Folders are single piece of paper folded once or twice, when opened it is presented in a sequential manner, usually they are prepared on offset or heavier paper. There are extension bulletins, which are booklets usually 12 to 20 pages with single topics that are discussed at length and in detail. They are primarily for extension workers, progressive farmers, schoolteachers and instructors in the colleges and also extension training centres.

Another type of media is **Folk media.** This can provide fresh and interesting programmes for the mass media making them more acceptable to both rural and urban audiences. These media are a source of popular entertainment for the rural audience, in addition to providing instruction and information. The role of the folk media in a country like ours is of paramount importance in enriching our culture and tradition as also disseminating information and educating our rural folk.

The different forms of folk media are Folk theatre forms, which are like Puppet shows and Tamasha of Maharashra, Nautanki of Punjab, Yakshgan, Keerthana, Harikatha and veedhinatakam from the South India.

Folk songs and dances like Hindustani, Karnatak, Khawwali types of music and Bharathanatyam, Kuchipudi, Manipuri, Odissi, Bhangda type of dances.

Communication can also conveyed through story telling from the elderly people, munadis as announcements in the villages and also through wall paintings etc.

Coming to the another type Electronic media, which includes motion pictures, i.e. cinema and different types of videos. Electronic channels range from the electronic mail to the television and from the telephone to videoconferencing. The obvious advantages of these media are speed and reach. They can cover more distance more quickly than it is possible with traditional means of conveying information.

Among the electronic media telephone was the first electronic channel to gain wide acceptance for business use. These services expand the utility of the telephone through answering voice mail, telephone conferencing, portable phones, pagers, and other devices designed to extend the speed and reach of the telephone as a communication device. Telephones can also be intrusive. The Rural telecommunication networks are powerful communication, information and knowledge sharing tools. They can bring new information resources for rural people and open communication channels to facilitate dialogue and exchange information between them and their colleagues, friends and organizations. They can also provide many services for rural people to overcome the effects of distance, isolation and equitable levels of services for them such as agricultural, health and education services.

Next electronic form of communication is through Radio, which is very effective means of broadcasting information to many people at once. For this reason, radio is a form of mass communication that has made inroads into the distant rural homes in developing countries. Even the Farm Forum Programme which involves community listening, discussion and feedback to the source covers only a handful of people, who often do not work in the fields and so they are not much knowledgeable also about the ground realities.

Next one is Television. This is the mass media, which is really dynamic in nature and very effective of broadcasting information to many people at once and also it is audio- visual in nature. It involves advertising and also information and education. Here it also involves training programmes, education and video conferencing through television. It provides a fairly effective substitute for face-to-face communication when time, distance, cost of travel would make face-to-face communication difficult.

Coming to Internet it is a network of networks and also it is a group of two or more networks which are interconnected. It is large collection of World Wide Web, which are interlinked together. Presently several lakhs of computers are interconnected with each other to share and exchange information. Email has recently become the most common form of business communication, substituting for letters, memos, and many telephone calls. People use internet to find general information through World Wide Web about a subject and also to access information which is not easily available everywhere.

Electronic conferencing, which is a very good electronic media helping in eliminating the problems of storing and retrieving information by categorizing subjects by topics or *threads.* The access to such conferences can also be easily restricted to qualified individuals, making them useful for discussions of proprietary matters, they are asynchronous in nature, allowing sender and receiver to access the information when convenient.

Another form of electronic media is advertising. This is a mass communication process where the transmission of information by the manufacturer or seller of a product or service to modify or stimulate the behavior of the buyer to buy a particular product or service. **This** can be in any form of presentation such as sign, symbol or illustration, in print media, or a commercial on radio or television or also any poster.

Cinema: cinema was a simple means of mechanical recording, preserving and reproducing moving visual images later transformed by its own type of communication. Films can be used for variety of purposes such as entertainment, education, persuasion, changing motivation and opinions. It can be conveyed through films that are retained better due to its reality element, comedy, drama, suspense, science fiction, or horror. They allow for a creative production approach. It is possible to make different language and cultural versions of a film.

CHAPTER VI

TYPES OF AUDIO VISUAL AIDS

Audio visual aids can be classified into three categories:

1. Audio aids
2. Visual aids
3. Audio-Visual aids

Audio aids are communication aids which provide information that we hear. Such information is received through ears. They include Radio, tape recorders, telephone and public address systems.

Radio: Radio is known to be the most effective mass media for communicating agricultural information. It can easily be used in the rural setting. It has been recommended by communication researchers and extension experts as an inexpensive medium for reaching a good majority of rural dwellers in many developing countries.

Tape Recorder helps information to be disseminated to the farmers can be recorded on audio tapes or cassettes with the aid of a tape recorder. This can then be played for the farmers in their villages conveniently at their own time.

A public address system is an electronic sound amplification and distribution system with a microphone, amplifier and loudspeakers, used to allow a person to address a large public in general meetings, seminars, workshops and training programmes.

Visual Aids are the instructional devices through which the message can only be seen not heard. The visual aids are starting from black board or chalk board to today's digital displays and LCD projectors which are used for advertising and social marketing. These are the various visual aids which are classified into two categories, Non projected and Projected.

Under the Non-Projected visual aids which are used for display in the common places for communication.

1. ***Posters:*** Poster is a placard displayed in a public place with the purpose of creating awareness amongst the people. So the job of the poster is to stop the hurriedly passing persons, thrust the message upon them quickly and lead them to action immediately or eventually.
2. ***Charts:*** Charts are the diagrammatic representation of facts or ideas, visual symbols for summarizing, comparing, contrasting and performing other services in explaining subject matter that can help to communicate difficult, dull subject in an interesting way.

They can be in many kinds like bar charts, pie charts, flow charts, tree charts, overlay charts, strip tease charts and suspense charts and also pictographs.

1. ***Flannel graph:*** This is also called Khaddergraph. Pieces of flannel felt or sand paper, will be bat having rough surfaces or nap will stick to another piece of flannel stretched on a firm flat surface called a "flannel board".
2. ***Flash cards:*** These are the series of cards which when presented before the audience in proper sequence, tell a complete story. The size depends upon the number of audience present and it is accompanied by a verbal commentary. The extension worker or the student, who wants to use them, holds them in hand and flashes before the audience one after the other.
3. There are also three-dimensional visual aids and these three-dimensional visual aids are good substitutes for real objects. On account of several reasons may not be possible to bring the real objects in the classroom. So, these three dimensional aids are such as models, specimen, mockups and diorama, aid in the instruction for bringing them into the classroom and also help in better understanding to the student.

Coming to the Projected visual aids: Any visual aid which is used for magnification of image on a screen in dark or semi dark conditions can be called projected visual aid. When combined with recorded or on the spot commentary, they prove to be useful in a large number of situations. Like all other visual and audio-visual aids, they are only aids which cannot be safely assumed that they alone can do the entire work of teaching. They have some specific limitations. They require specific equipment for their display. The equipment is highly costly, needs meticulous care and attention and in many cases, call for special training also in handling and maintenance.

There are many factors that can affect the quality of projected images. Three of these are particularly important:

1. The Kind of screen,
2. The placement of audience in relation to the screen,
3. The size of image and its brightness.

Understanding these factors contributes more effective preparation and use of projected aids. The limitations however, do not lessen the importance of these aids or visuals wherever suitable, because they are definite advantages. The important projected visual aids are slide projector, overhead projector and opaque projector.

1. **Slide projector:** An ordinary slide projector has a frame containing two slits into which slides are put for focusing. They are manually or automatically managed with the help of a remote and replaced manually with the help of a hand also.
2. **Overhead projector:** is projected over the head of the speaker on the screen. This is accomplished by overhead projector through showing drawing, lettering or with the help of a transparent sheets which are also called as transparencies'. The strong light is passed through and it is converged by a lens and reflected by a mirror held at an angle and it will be in turn seen

on the screen.

3. **Opaque projector:** A large – aperture projector is used to project opaque materials also known as Epidiascope. Pictures, drawings, diagrams from books directly can be shown on the sheets of paper and also they will be directly shown on the screen without any preparations.

CHAPTER VII

MEDIA COMBINATION

These are the media which are used singly or in combination, taking the following factors into consideration

The first and foremost is the teaching objective:

The type of behaviour change you want to bring about, like gaining information or changing attitude or learning some skill should be:

- Pertinent to learner's needs.
- Applicable to their real life situations.
- Well organized and presented logically & clearly.
- Consistent with the overall objectives and
- Challenging, satisfying and significant to the learners also.

The nature of the subject matter is the second factor, which is the content or topic, which should be taught. It should proceed from

- Known to unknown
- Simple to complex
- Concrete to abstract
- Definite to indefinite.
- Particular to general.

Regarding the third factor the nature of audience: There can be individual differences in the audience like age level, educational level, interest, experience, knowledge of the subject and intelligence. In an effective learning situation, we are supposed to make use of the learner to make them as a central position of the learning situation and all efforts should be directed towards them.

The audience always should:

- Be capable of learning.
- Have interest in the subject.
- Have need for the information offered.
- Be able to use the information once it is gained.

Regarding relative cost of the various media, it need not necessarily be expensive; it also should be concerned with the skill in using the several aids, skill in selection, preparation and use also.

- The instructor should make use of indigenous materials, when the teaching aid she/ he would like to use that is not available.

- Media are the best motivators. The students with more interest and zeal, they will be motivated towards all these audio-visual media and the attention also will be called for very easily.
- They will be acting as Antidote to the disease of verbal instruction. They help in giving clear concepts and thus help in bringing accuracy in learning.
- It is beyond doubt that the first-hand experience is the best type of educational experience. So, it is neither practicable nor desirable to provide such experience to pupils. So vicarious experience will also be provided through audio-visual media.
- Audio-Visual media give variety and provide different tools in the hands of the teacher
- Many visual aids offer opportunities to students and manipulate the things.
- They contribute to increase retention as they stimulate response of the whole organism to the situation in which learning takes place
- The use of audio visual media enable the teacher to follow the maxims of teaching, a concrete to abstract, known to unknown and learning by doing.
- The attention is the true factor in any process of teaching and learning also and also in instruction. These media help the teacher in providing proper environment for capturing as well

as sustaining the attention and interest of the students in the classroom work.

- They are also Helpful in fixing up new learning also. Based upon the needs of the learner.
- Lots of time and energy also being saved both by the teachers and by the learners and audience also on account of use of visual media and most of the concepts and phenomena may be easily clarified, understood and assimilated through their use.
- The use of audio-visual media provides a touch of reality to the learning situation.
- They are vivid in nature during the learning process happening.
- It also meets the different individual difference of the audience and it is ear-oriented and some can be helped through visual demonstrations, while others learn better by doing also. The use of a variety of audio-visual media helps in meeting the needs of different types of students.
- It also encourages to a healthy classroom interaction, where a wide variety of stimuli, provision of active participation of the students, and various experiences encouraging for different activities also will be helping in interaction for the effective realization of teaching –learning objectives.
- It also helps in Spread of education on a mass scale also. This can be possible through the radio and television in providing the opportunities for learning.
- This gives place for listening of facts and observe demonstrations and phenomena which cultivate scientific temper.

Coming to the Problems of Use of Audio-Visual media

- Mainly first and foremost thing is the Indifference of students. The judicious use of aids arouses interest but when used without a definite purpose they lose their significance and importance.
- Even due to the absence of proper planning and lethargy of the teacher, without proper preparation, correct presentation,

appropriate application and discussion the essential follow-up work and the aids do not provide or prove their full usefulness.

- Lack of finances are not enabling teachers to do their best. So that also may become one of the problem in showing the audio-visual media in best way.
- Absence of different facilities just like electricity and place, all these things also creates a difficult situation for the teachers in training different people and workers.
- The Language barrier also is a big barrier coming in the way just like mostly if they are in various other languages it is difficult for the rural people in development communication to grasp what is being taught to them.
- Last but not the least Selection based on local needs. Little attention is paid in the production of audio-visual media to the local sociological, psychological and pedagogical aspects catering to the local needs of the people.

CHAPTER VIII

MEANING, HISTORY AND IMPORTANCE OF VISUAL COMMUNICATION

The communication which is done through a visual aid is called ***visual communication.*** Such as facial expression, gesture, eye contact, signals, map, chart, poster etc. it also includes graphic design, illustration and animation, books, print, magazines, screen-based media, interactive web design, short film, design for advertising, promotion, corporate identity and packaging design etc.Visual presentation of information and data is having an increasing impact on our practical life. In spite of having impact on our life, visual communication is not alone sufficient for exchanging information. For example to indicate 'danger' we use red sign, to indicate 'no smoking'; we use an image showing a lighted cigarette with across mark on it etc.

The Cro-Magnons was found in the history that the Cro-Magnons form the earliest known European examples of Homo sapiens, from 40,000 years ago, chromosomally descending from populations of the Middle East. Cro-Magnons lived from about 40,000 to 10,000 years ago in the Upper Paleolithic period of the Pleistocene epoch. When they arrived in Europe about 40,000 years ago, they brought with them sculpture, engraving, painting, body ornamentation, music and the painstaking decoration of utilitarian objects.

Cave or rock paintings are paintings painted on cave or rock walls and ceilings, usually dating to prehistoric times. Rock paintings are made since the Upper Paleolithic, 40,000 years ago. It is widely believed that the paintings are the work of respected elders or shamans.

Now we will discuss about Pictograms, ideograms and logograms.

Pictogram: A Pictogram or pictograph is a symbol representing a concept, object, activity, place or event by illustration. Pictography is a form of writing whereby ideas are transmitted through drawing. It is the basis of cuneiform and hieroglyphs. They were used by various ancient cultures all over the world since around 9000 BC and began to develop into logographic writing systems around 5000 BC. Pictograms are still in use as the main medium of written communication in some non-literate cultures in Africa, The Americas, and Oceania, and are often used as simple symbols by most contemporary cultures.

An ideogram or ideograph is a graphical symbol that represents an idea, rather than a group of letters arranged according to the phonemes of a spoken language, as is done in alphabetic languages. Examples of ideograms include way finding signage, in airports and other environments where many people may not be familiar with the language of the place they are in, as well as Arabic numerals and mathematical notation, which are used worldwide regardless of how they are pronounced in different languages. The term "ideogram" is commonly used to describe logographic writing systems such as Egyptian hieroglyphs and Chinese characters. However, symbols in logographic systems generally represent words or morphemes rather than pure ideas.

A logogram, or logograph, is a single grapheme which represents a word or a morpheme. This stands in contrast to other writing systems, such as alphabets, where each symbol primarily represents a sound or a combination of sounds.

The history of the alphabet starts in ancient Egypt. The first pure alphabets emerged around 2000 BC in Ancient Egypt, as a representation of language developed by Semitic workers in Egypt, but by then alphabetic principles had already been inculcated into Egyptian hieroglyphs for a millennium. Most other alphabets in the world today either descended from this one discovery, **or** were directly inspired by its design, including the Phoenician alphabet and the Greek alphabet.

This was one of the darkest periods known to mankind. InMedieval Europe, Pestilence and plague, darkness and fear, witch-hunts and illiteracy roam the land. It is a world where most people seldom leave their place of birth for any distance longer than 10 miles, where few people even live beyond the age of 30. In this inhospitable milieu, secluded in the scriptoria of cold monasteries, under the light of feeble oil lamps, mittened against the biting cold; some of the greatest book designers that ever lived, created some of the most beautiful books the world has ever seen. We call these beautiful books Illuminated Manuscripts.

Let's now talk about Incunabula. Incunabula is a book, single sheet, or image that was printed — not handwritten — before the year 1501 in Europe. These are usually very rare and fragile items whose nature can only be verified by experts. The origin of the word is the Latin incunabula for "swaddling clothes", used by extension for the infancy or early stages of something. The first recorded use of incunabula as a printing term is in a pamphlet by Bernard von Mallinckrodt, "Of the rise and progress of the typographic art", published in Cologne in 1639, which includes the phrase prima typographicae incunabula, "the first infancy of printing". The term came to denote the printed books themselves from the late 17th century.

There are two types of incunabula:

- Xylographic (made from a single carved or sculpted block for each page) and the
- Typographic (made with movable type on a printing press in the style of Johann Gutenberg).

Many authors reserve the term incunabulum for the typographic ones only. The end date for identifying a book as an incunabulum is convenient, but was chosen arbitrarily. It does not reflect any notable developments in the printing process around the year 1500. Incunabula usually refer to the earliest printed books, completed at a time when some books were still being hand-copied. The gradual spread of printing ensured that there was great variety in the texts chosen for printing and the styles in which they appeared. Many early typefaces were modeled on local forms of writing or derived from the various European forms of Gothic script, but there were also some derived from documentary scripts (such as most of Caxton's types), and, particularly in Italy, types modeled on humanistic hands. These humanistic typefaces are often used today, barely modified, in digital form.

Visual communication is communication through a visual aid and is described as the conveyance of ideas and information in forms that can be read or looked upon. Visual communication is part or whole relies on vision, and is primarily presented or expressed with two dimensional images, it includes: signs, typography, drawing, graphic design, illustration, industrial Design, Advertising, Animation, colour and electronic resources. It also explores the idea that a visual message accompanying text has a greater power to inform, educate, or persuade a person or audience.

Visual communication is through visual aid. The evaluation of a good visual communication design is mainly based on measuring comprehension by the audience, not on personal aesthetic and/or artistic preference as there are no universally agreed-upon principles of beauty and ugliness. Excluding two dimensional images, there are other ways to express information visually - gestures and body language, animation, and film. Visual communication by e-mail, a textual medium, is commonly expressed with ASCII art, emotions, and embedded digital images.

The term 'visual presentation' is used to refer to the actual presentation of information through a visible medium such as text or images. Recent research in the field has focused on web design and graphically-oriented usability. Graphic designers also use methods of visual communication in their professional practice. Visual communication on the World Wide Web is perhaps the most important form of communication that takes place while users are surfing the Internet. When experiencing the web, one uses the eyes as the primary sense, and therefore the visual presentation of a website is very important for users to understand the message or of the communication taking place.

Visual communication uses artistic license to communicate thoughts and ideas through sight. People skilled in visual communications commonly work in advertising, Web design, journalism and publishing, and in many cases in own their studios to teach their craft. They use simple and advanced techniques to get their message across – everything from pencils to computers. Most people get a college degree or attend a specialized school to learn their craft.

- Graphic designers plan and create marketing materials that communicate visually. They work in a variety of settings, including publishing companies, advertising firms and corporations where they assist with advertising campaigns and business promotions. Graphic designers also develop brochures, press packets and fundraising programs. Some choose to work alone and freelance for clients. Many graphic designers earn college degrees and stay current on the latest software programs.
- Artists work in many creative fields, such as advertising, public relations and set design. Others are employed as cartoonists, illustrators, art directors and interior decorators. While many artists work for someone else, many still create their own artwork and sell it to supplement their income. Many also teach in schools and give private lessons. Artists often specialize in sculpture, watercolor, oil, illustration, pastels, pencils, pens, clay or computer animation.
- Photographers tell stories with their pictures to capture and to record major events for future generations. Photographers spend years learning their craft. Photographers typically earn a college degree or complete specialized training at a photography school or art institute. Many are self-employed and earn a living photographing individuals and special family occasions, such as weddings. Others work as photojournalists or crime scene photographers affiliated with a police department.

- Professionals skilled in multimedia have solid knowledge and understanding of all forms of visual communication in order to produce cutting-edge communication pieces for a client or business. For example, in order to put together an engaging company website to attract page hits and customers, a Web page must contain high quality photography, attractive graphic design, original artwork and, in some cases, an attention-grabbing video.

Visual aids are often used to help audiences of informative and persuasive speeches understand the topic being presented. Visual aids can play a large role in how the audience understands and takes in information that is presented. There are many different types of visual aids that range from handouts to PowerPoints. The type of visual aid a speaker uses depends on their preference and the information they are trying to present. Each type of visual aid has pros and cons that must be evaluated to ensure it will be beneficial to the overall presentation. Before incorporating visual aids into speeches, the speaker should understand that if used incorrectly, the visual will not be an aid, but a distraction. Planning ahead is important when using visual aids. It is necessary to choose a visual aid that is appropriate for the material and audience. The purpose of the visual aid is to enhance the presentation.

- **Chalkboard or whiteboard:** Chalkboards and whiteboards are very useful visual aids, particularly when more advanced types of media are unavailable. They are cheap and also allow for much flexibility. The use of chalkboards or whiteboards is convenient, but they are not a perfect visual aid. Often, using this medium as an aid can create confusion or boredom. Particularly if a student who is not familiar with how to properly use visual aids attempts to draw on a board while they are speaking, they detract time and attention from their actual speech.

- **Poster board:** A poster is a very simple and easy visual aid. Posters can display charts, graphs, pictures, or illustrations. The biggest drawback of using a poster as a visual aid is that often a poster can appear unprofessional. Since a poster board paper is relatively flimsy, often the paper will bend or fall over. The best way to present a poster is to hang it up or tape it to a wall.

- **Handouts:** Handouts can also display charts, graphs, pictures, or illustrations. An important aspect of the use of a handout is that a person can keep a handout with them long after the presentation is over. This can help the person better remember what was discussed. Passing out handouts, however, can be extremely distracting. Once a handout is given out, it might potentially be difficult to bring back your audience's attention. The person who receives the handout might be tempted to read what is on the paper, which will keep them from listening to what the speaker is saying. If using a handout, the speaker distributes the hand out right before you reference it. Distributing handouts is acceptable in a lecture that is an hour or two, but in a short lecture of five to ten minutes, a handout should not be used.

- A video can be a great visual aid and attention grabber, however, a video is not a replacement for an actual speech. There are several potential drawbacks to playing a video during a speech or lecture. First, if a video is playing that includes audio, the speaker will not be able to talk. Also, if the video is very exciting and interesting, it can make what the speaker is saying appear boring and uninteresting. The key to showing a video during a presentation is to make sure to transition smoothly into the video and to only show very short clips.

- There are several types of projectors. These include slide projectors, PowerPoint presentations, overhead projectors, and computer projectors. Slide projectors are the oldest form of projector, and are no longer used. Power Point presentations are very popular and are used often. Overhead projectors are still used but are somewhat inconvenient to use. In order to use an overhead projector, a transparency must be made of whatever is being projected onto the screen. This takes time and costs money. Computer or LCD projectors are the most technologically advanced projectors. When using a LCD projector, pictures and slides are easily taken right from a computer either online or from a saved file and are blown up and shown on a large screen. Though LCD projectors are technologically advanced, they are not always completely reliable because technological breakdowns are not uncommon of the computers of today.

- PowerPoint presentations can be an extremely useful visual aid, especially for longer presentations. For five- to ten-minute presentations, it is probably not worth the time or effort to put together a PowerPoint. For longer presentations, however, PowerPoints can be a great way to keep the audience engaged and keep the speaker on track. A potential drawback of using a PowerPoint is that it usually takes a lot of time and energy to put together. There is also the possibility of a computer malfunction, which can mess up the flow of a presentation.

Modern world became more visualized in every aspect due to the high influence of media. Visual communication is the communication in which pictures, colors and graphics are used. A skull and two cross bones shows the meaning of danger. So, **visual communication** is a communication where the ideas and information can be read or viewed through the means of a visual aid.

Let's take a look at the Advantages of visual communication

Now-a-days, most of the business organizations are using visual techniques to present the information. It is becoming very popular day by day. Visual presentation is beneficial for many reasons.

1. **Effective for illiterate receiver**: If the receivers are illiterate, the visual communication will be more effective to exchange information. They can easily understand the information that is presented visually.
2. **Helps in oral communication**: Visual techniques can be used with oral communication. Oral communication becomes more meaningful if graphs, pictures and diagrams are used with it.
3. **Easy explanation**: Everyone can explain the meaning of it very easily. Easy explanation has made the visual techniques more popular.
4. **Simple presentation**: Complex information, data and figures can be easily presented very simply on graphs, pictures and diagrams.
5. Another advantage of visual communication is, it **Helps in quick decision.** Visual communication helps to take quick decision. So management prefers visual techniques to communicate with others.
6. **Popularity** is another advantage of Visual Communication. Visual communication is very much popular because people do not like much speech and long explanation rather than a chart of a diagram.
7. **Other** advantage of visual communication, Artful presentation, Ads impact to the information, quicker understanding.

Let us now discuss about disadvantages of visual communication:

1. The first disadvantage of visual communication is, it is very **Costly.** The visual methods of communication are more costlier than those of other methods. To draw maps, charts, diagram is

costly affair. That is why only large company or organization can use this technique.

2. **Complex presentation**: Sometimes visual presentation of information becomes complex. The receivers cannot understand the meaning of the presentation.
3. **Another disadvantage of visual communication, Incomplete method.** This technique is considered as an incomplete method. Visual presentation is not sufficient to communicate effectively and clearly but also it can be successfully used with oral communication.
4. **Wastage of time**: Sometimes visual techniques take much time to communicate. Whereas oral communication takes no time to exchange information.
5. **The other disadvantage of visual communication is Difficult to understand.** Difficult to understand and requires a lot of repetitions in visual communication. Since it uses gestures, facial expressions, eye contact, touch etc. for communicating with others which may not be understandable for the simple and foolish people.
6. **Visual communication can be a Problem for general readers.** General people does not prefers to communicate through visual communication with others. Sometimes it cannot create an impression upon people or listeners. It is less influential and cannot be used everywhere.
7. **The Other disadvantages are** Ambiguity, situational problem, delays in taking decision.

CHAPTER IX

FORMS OF VISUAL MATERIAL IN COMMUNICATION

Visual communication is communication through a visual aid and is described as the conveyance of ideas and information in forms that can be read or looked upon. Visual communication in part or whole relies on vision, and is primarily presented or expressed with two dimensional images, it includes: signs, typography, drawing, graphic design, illustration, Industrial Design, Advertising, Animation colour and electronic resources. It also explores the idea that a visual message accompanying text has a greater power to inform, educate, or persuade a person or audience. Visual communication takes place through pictures, graphs and charts, as well as through signs, signals and symbols. It may be used either independently or as an adjunct to the other methods of communication.

Now we will move on to the types of visual aids:

Objects: The use of objects as visual aids involves bringing the actual object to demonstrate on during the speech. For example, a speech about tying knots would be more effective by bringing in a rope. The use of the actual object is often necessary when demonstrating how to do something so that the audience can fully understand procedure. Some objects are too large or unavailable for a speaker to bring with them.

Next we move on to Models: Models are representations of another object that serve to demonstrate that object when use of the real object is ineffective for some reason. Examples include human skeletal systems, the solar system, or architecture. Models can serve as substitutes that provide a better example of the real thing to the audience when the object being spoken about is of an awkward size or composure for use in the demonstration.

Sometimes a model may take away from the reality of what is being spoken about. For example, the vast size of the solar system cannot be seen from a model, and the actual composure of a human body cannot be seen from a dummy.

Next we move on to Graphs: Graphs are used to visualize relationships between different quantities. Various types are used as visual aids, including bar graphs, line graphs, pie graphs, and scatter plots. Graphs help the audience to visualize statistics so that they can make a greater impact than just listing them verbally would. Graphs can easily become cluttered during use in a speech by including too much detail, overwhelming the audience and making the graph ineffective.

Maps: Maps show geographic areas that are of interest to the speech. They often are used as aids when speaking of differences between geographical areas or showing the location of something. When maps are simple and clear, they can be used to effectively make points about certain areas. For example, a map showing the building site for a new hospital could show its close location to key neighborhoods, or a map could show the differences in distribution of AIDS victims in North American and African countries. Inclusion of too much detail on a map can cause the audience to lose focus on the key point being made. Also, if the map is disproportional or unrealistic, it may prove ineffective for the point being made.

Tables: Tables are columns and rows that organize words, symbols, and/or data. Good tables are easy to understand. They are a good way to compare facts and to gain a better overall understanding of the topic being discussed.

Photographs: Photographs are good tools to make or emphasize a point or to explain a topic. For example, when explaining the shanty-towns in a third world country it would be beneficial to show a picture of one so the reader can have a better understanding of how those people live.

Drawings or diagrams: Drawings or diagrams can be used when photographs do not show exactly what the speaker wants to show or explain. It could also be used when a photograph is too detailed. For example, a drawing or diagram of the circulatory system throughout the body is a lot more effective than a picture of a cadaver showing the circulatory system. If not drawn correctly a drawing can look sloppy and be ineffective. This type of drawing will appear unprofessional.

Module 2: Principles in designing visual material

Visual communication contains image aspects. The interpretation of images is subjective and to understand the depth of meaning, or multiple meanings, communicated in an image requires analysis. Images can be analysed through many perspectives.

Personal perspective

When a viewer has an opinion about an image based on their personal thoughts. Personal response depends on the viewer's thoughts and values individually. This might be sometimes in conflict with cultural values. Also when a viewer has viewed an image with a personal perspective, it is hard to change the view of the image on the viewer, and the image can even be seen in other ways.

Historical perspective

An image's view can be arising from the history of the use media. Through times sort images have been changed, because the use of different or new media. For example: The result of using the computer to edit images (e.g. Photoshop) is quite different when comparing images that are made and edited by craft.

Technical perspective

When the view of an image is influenced by the use of lights, position and the presentation of the image. The right use of light, position and presentation of the image can improve the view of the image. It makes the image looks better than the reality.

Ethical perspective

From this perspective, the maker of the image, the viewer and the image itself must be responsible morally and ethically to the image. This perspective is also categorized in six categories, i.e.

categorical imperative, utilitarianism, hedonism, golden mean, golden rule and veil of ignorance.

Next we move on to Cultural perspective

Symbolization is an important definition for this perspective. Cultural perspective involves identity of symbols. The uses of words that are related with the image, the use of heroes in the image, etc. are the symbolization of the image. The cultural perspective can also be seen as the semiotic perspective.

Critical perspective

The view of images in the critical perspective is when the viewers criticize the images, but the critics have been made in interests of the society, although an individual makes the critics. This way this perspective differs from the personal perspective.

Principles in graphic reproduction

Design Elements: Design elements are the basic units of graphic reproduction i.e. a painting, drawing, design or other visual pieces and include:

Color: Colors play a large role in the elements of design with the color wheel being used as a tool, and color theory providing a body of practical guidance to color mixing and the visual impacts of specific color combination.

Uses

- Color can aid organization to develop a color strategy and stay consistent with those colors.
- It can give emphasis to create a hierarchy to the piece of art.
- It is also important to note that color choices in design change meaning within cultural contexts.
- For example, white is associated with purity in some cultures while it is associated with death in others.

Attributes

- Hue

- Values, tints and shades of colors that are created by adding black to a color for a shade and white for a tint. Creating a tint or shade of color reduces the saturation.
- Saturation gives a color brightness or dullness, and by doing this it makes the color more vibrant than before.

Shape: A shape is defined as a two or more dimensional area that stands out from the space next to or around it due to a defined or implied boundary, or because of differences of value, color, or texture. All objects are composed of shapes and all other 'Elements of Design' are shapes in some way.

Categories

- Mechanical Shapes or Geometric Shapes are the shapes that can be drawn using a ruler or compass. Mechanical shapes, whether simple or complex, produce a feeling of control or order.
- Organic Shapes are freehand drawn shapes that are complex and normally found in nature. Organic shapes produce a natural feel.

Texture: Meaning the way a surface feels or is perceived to feel. Texture can be added to attract or repel interest to an element, depending on the pleasantness of the texture.

Types of texture

- Tactile texture is the actual three-dimension feel of the surface that can be touched. Painter can use impasto to build peaks and create texture.
- Visual texture is the illusion of the surfaces peaks and valleys, like the tree pictured. Any texture shown in a photo is a visual texture, meaning the paper is smooth no matter how rough the image perceives it to be.

Most textures have a natural touch but still seem to repeat a motif in some way. Regularly repeating a motif will result in a texture appearing as a pattern.

Space: In design, space is concerned with the area deep within the moment of designated design; the design will take place on. For a two-dimensional design, space concerns creating the illusion of a third dimension on a flat surface

- Overlap is the effect where objects appear to be on top of each other. This illusion makes the top element look closer to the observer. There is no way to determine the depth of the space, only the order of closeness.
- Shading adds gradiation marks to make an object of a two-dimensional surface seem three-dimensional.
- Highlight, Transitional Light, Core of the Shadow, Reflected Light, and Cast Shadow give an object a three-dimensional look.
- Linear Perspective is the concept relating to how an object seems smaller the farther away it gets.
- Atmospheric Perspective is based on how air acts as a filter to change the appearance of distant objects.

Form: Form may be described as any three-dimensional object. Form can be measured, from top to bottom, i.e. height, side to side (width), and from back to front (depth). Form is also defined by light and dark. It can be defined by the presence of shadows on surfaces or faces of an object. There are two types of form, geometric (man-made) and natural (organic form). Form may be created by the combining of two or more shapes. It may be enhanced by tone, texture and color. It can be illustrated or constructed.

Principles of Designing Visual Material:

A simple set of principles that help novice designers create better looking visual documents. We will have to focus on these principles, which happen to form a rather memorable acronym, i.e. **CRAP — Contrast, Repetition, Alignment, and Proximity**, each of which is explained in the following sections.

Principle of Contrast: If you have ever tried to view a projected PowerPoint slideshow where the instructor used light text on a light colored background, you have experienced a very common violation of the principle of CONTRAST. Digital projectors often wash out document colors, especially if the screen or display surface (such as a wall) does not have a highly reflective coating. Poor color selection, a weak projector, and ambient lighting can transform what was easily readable on a computer monitor into completely illegible content when projected. One solution to this very common problem is to make ample use of contrast where appropriate. Dark colored text is obviously much more readable on a light colored background, and vice-versa, but contrast can also be created in many other ways. For example, consider contrasting:

1. Large type with small type
2. Bold text with plain text
3. Caps with non-caps
4. Thin lines with thick lines,
5. Large graphics with small graphics
6. Changes in element positioning

An important point to remember regarding the principle of Contrast is to BE OBVIOUS. Don't try to create contrast with element styles that are too similar to distinguish easily. That's why light green text isn't readable on yellow backgrounds, why 12 point text doesn't look much different than 14 point text, and why a circle shape doesn't create emphasis near an oval shape. If you plan to use contrast, don't be wishy-washy!

Principle of Repetition: In order to generate visual consistency some page elements or element formatting should be repeated throughout the entire document. The intent of this principle is to facilitate viewer eye movement across a document to ensure appropriate message sequencing, and establish a motif to reinforce the messages. Some of the most common repetitions are:

1. Fonts or font styles
2. Headers or titles

3. Color schemes
4. Spatial relationships
5. Graphic types or shapes

Principle of Alignment: The principle of ALIGNMENT suggests that every element in a document is positioned deliberately, and is connected in some way to at least one other element. By using invisible axes to align multiple elements, a designer can establish a framing structure that facilitates eye movement and improving message sequencing.

Principle of Proximity: The principle of PROXIMITY is derived from decades of research on short-term memory theory, which has established that most student readers can maintain no more than seven separate ideas in working memory. Good document designs therefore, should group related elements near each other in order to imply logical relationships and reduce the major ideas into fewer than seven subunits to facilitate comprehension by obviating the need to process each element individually.

Theory into Practice—Design ---a Sign: Microsoft Publisher is representative of a class of software applications designed to create these labels, signs, flyers, cards, nametags, posters, newsletters and other desktop publishing (DTP) documents that help teachers organize their classrooms and resources. The core features in Publisher go well beyond Word with the addition of enhanced drawing and layout tools that allow users to manipulate text, shape, line, art and photo objects with significant precision.

Barriers in effective visual communication

Although visual aids help communication, there is also evidence to show that they can create barriers to effective communication. Usually we create these barriers when we give insufficient thought to the planning and use of the visual aids for promoting better communication and more effective learning. The following points outline some important factors to be kept in mind.

Decide what we require of the visual aid: Aids should be used as an important and integral part of the learning process. They should be used

- to create interest;
- to help learners understand information being given;
- to help them recall major points that they remember; and
- to help them develop a mental perception of the information.

Plan the visual aids carefully Good visual aids do not appear by chance - or rarely so. Usually a great deal of thought goes into their creation. It is advisable to prepare a rough sketch and ask the following questions:

- Is it what is really wanted?
- Is it as simple and bold as we can make it?
- Can they build the information step-by-step to control what the audience is looking at?
- Is it as interesting as we can make it?
-
- Is the visual neat in appearance?

Using a visual aid: If much effort has been used to produce good visual aids, then we should use them to their best advantage.

Here are few points worth remembering:

- Do not obstruct the view of the audience.
- The visual must be well placed.
- Do not read a visual word by word to the audience.
- Do not wave a pointer in front of the visual.
- Do not talk to the visual.

Next we move on to Visibility: With all visual aids it is vital that everyone should see it. Adopting the Rule of Seven ensures this, which is

- Not more than seven lines on an acetate sheet

- Not more than seven words in a line; and
- Size of letters 7 mm
- In addition, colour can be used to highlight various parts of the aid

Whether you're presenting a new product idea or information, the way you communicate your information can greatly impact how well your audience understands. Your communication style and technique can also heavily influence whether your audience supports the ideas and information you present. Whether you use written or verbal communication, visual aids can enhance your presentation and help you overcome barriers of communication.

Information Processing

Since people process and digest information differently, combining visual aids with a presentation or document can present the audience with various ways to receive the information. As a result, you increase your chances of having the audience understand what is being communicated. Some people understand things better orally; others prefer the written word, while others prefer a graph or table.

Information Overload

A common communication barrier employers and employees face when presenting or receiving information is that too much information is presented at once. When this happens, it's hard to determine which information is most important and relevant to their tasks and responsibilities. Visual aids, such as graphs and flow charts, can condense large chunks of information into the most important portions.

Information Retention

If you are standing in front of a group presenting information for 30 minutes, the likelihood of them retaining the information is slim, especially if the audience has a hard time concentrating or is uninterested in your information. Using visual aids, along with verbal or written forms of communication, can help the audience retain the information.

Language Barriers

Language barriers are a common communication barrier, especially as the workforce becomes more diverse. Nonnative speakers may not fully understand The information during a verbal presentation; however, with visual aids they can perhaps use deductive reasoning to grasp your main ideas.

Limited Time

A picture is still worth 1,000 words; thus, visual aids save time in conveying ideas. This is true whether an employee is preparing a written report for a busy executive or that executive has to present information to a group. Visual aids provide a quick way to get the main points of the sales pitch or idea for product packaging.

CHAPTER X

NEWS

NEWS is the one of the best known commodities in today's world. Everybody who understands a language and has access to mass media recognizes it. The concept of NEWS must have existed even before the beginning of the era of mass media. "Mass media" in India is a part of the Indian media which aims to reach a wide audience.

NEWS Definition: "NEWS is an account of a recent event or opinion which is important or interesting".

KINDS OF NEWS

News can be divided on the basis of contents as:

1. International News;
2. National News;
3. Political News;
4. Accidents and Disasters;
5. News about Labour;
6. News about Crime and Violence; and
7. Sport News.

Besides, news can be categorized on the basis of priority as:

1. Hard News; and
2. Soft News.

Hard news is based on urgency of the news. In other words it is immediately conveyed to the people. It should reach people immediately. Priority is given to such news in the newspaper.

For example: Budget, Social welfare schemes, warning about cyclone and flood, come under this category of Hard News.

Soft news is published without any urgency. It is otherwise called secondary news. People evince less interest and importance to this kind of soft news.

For example: Association Meetings and Resolutions and news about General Knowledge.

News can be further divided on the **basis of expectation** as:

- Expected News.
- Unexpected News.

Some news is expected by the people. They are waiting for such news. **For example:** Budget Proposal and Parliament and State Legislature News come under expected news.

Unexpected news is called sudden news. Accidents happen unexpectedly; so also riots and communal clashes occur suddenly and unexpectedly. Such news is called unexpected news.

Spot news is what it says: news gathering on the spot, live, recent, immediate and fresh with the reporter being able to say: "I was right there!" spot news is not something that was expected or scheduled. It has an element of the exciting and the news.

<u>News gathering techniques</u>

There are four most commonly used methods in news gathering, which is, observation, telephone conversations, research and interviews.

OBSERVATION: Observation consists of your actually seeing an event take place and then reporting what you have seen in the form of a news story.

TELEPHONE CONVERSATIONS: The telephone plays an important role in your daily work as a journalist. It saves you time, legwork and it often enables you to reach people who are ordinarily too busy to see you in person.

RESEARCH: Research is nothing more than digging out information from files and reference works. Research is used to verify or amplify facts in news stories and to give depth to feature stories and magazine articles.

INTERVIEWS: About 90 percent of everything in a news story is based on some form of interviewing - either in person, by telephone, or occasionally, by correspondence.

TYPES OF INTERVIEWS

Interviews are as varied as the people who grant them, the journalists who conduct them and the news that suggests them. Rarely are interviews so mechanical that they can be reduced to standard formulas or categories. Several types, however, deserve special attention because they are the ones that occur most frequently. They are:

NEWS INTERVIEW - The news interview is based on "hard news," some event or development of current and immediate interest.

TELEPHONE INTERVIEW - The telephone interview, a modified version of the news interview, has a number of obvious advantages, and at the same time, it has several limitations that challenge a resourceful journalist.

CASUAL INTERVIEW. An accidental encounter between a journalist and a news source on the street or at a social gathering can often result in a tip that arouses the curiosity of a writer. A major news story may be the result after you do some digging.

PERSONALITY INTERVIEW. In the personality interview an effort is made to let the reader see the appearance, mannerisms, background and even the character of the subject.

SYMPOSIUM INTERVIEW. - From time to time, news developments of current interest require a journalist or a team of journalists to seek information not from one or two sources but from a dozen, or perhaps a hundred or more. In other instances, reactions and comments may result in a lively feature story.

NEWS CONFERENCE - In recent years, an increasingly popular phenomenon of journalism has developed -the news conference. One of the most potent forces in the public exchange of opinion between the people and their government. The news conference has been an important source of news.

NEWS AGENCIES IN INDIA THAT HELP IN NEWS GATHERING TO THE MEDIA:

Today, India has four main news agencies, i.e.

Press Trust of India (PTI) is the largest news agency in India. It is headquartered in New Delhi and is a nonprofit cooperative among more than 500 Indian newspapers and has more than 1,000 full-time employees. It provides news coverage and information of the region in both English and Hindi. Its corporate office is located at Sansad Marg, New Delhi and registered office in D N Road, Mumbai.

Indo-Asian News Service or IANS is a private Indian news agency: The IANS was founded by Indian American publisher Gopal Raju as the India Abroad News Service. It was later renamed the Indo-Asian News Service. The IANS has main offices located in Noida.

IANS reports about India with news, views and analyses about the country across a wide range of subjects. News, features and views from the subcontinent reach subscribers via the Internet.

United News of India (UNI) is a multilingual news agency in India. UNI is registered as a trust under the Indian Societies Registration Act. It is owned by the group of newspapers that have bought shares to run them. Currently, it is one of the important news agencies in India, supplying news in English, Hindi, and Urdu languages. Its news bureaus are present in all state capitals and major cities of India.

Next is the Hindustan Samachar: This is the first multilingual news agency of India. It is run by Hindusthan Samachar cooperative society formed under the Cooperative Society Act. It has 23 bureaus across the country and a News headquarters in New Delhi.

Next is Samachar Bharati: Samachar Bharti (SB) is a news agency based in India. It is headquartered in Bhopal and is a nonprofit cooperative among more than 500 Indian news paper. Its main focus is the production of independent news and analysis about events and processes affecting economic, social and political development.

Amongst all these news agencies, PTI and UNI have made a great impact in the distribution of national and international news in India.

Types of News stories and editorial

TYPES OF NEWS STORIES –

The curtain raiser: It is a story on what is likely to happen and not a report on what has happened. It raises the curtain to show what is on the stage and how the drama will unfold itself. It is based on past events and the reporter understands of what is likely to come on the strength of his information on what had happened in the past.

Crime reporting: There is tremendous public interest in crime stories. No newspaper can afford to ignore them without damage to its circulation and credibility. Crime reporting is a highly responsible and specialized job.

In depth reporting: Depth reporting is what makes readers aware of all aspects of a given subject by giving them all possible information, including background and atmosphere. Depth reporting treats a story with a kind of thoroughness of details and background that a 300-words story cannot. Depth reporting is simply good reporting with an eye for accuracy and detail.

Advocacy/Crusade reporting: The crusading understandably was for freedom. A crusade is not fought by writing one editorial or one news story. The obvious characteristics of a crusade are that it is concerned with the public good as seen by the editor. In conducting a crusade, the editor may bring all the ammunition he has to the battle editorials, in depth-reporting, investigation reporting, even cartoons.

Feature writing: A feature is expected to give the background to the news, which includes analysis, explanation and discussion. It should document facts, possible anticipate developments. Perception is a great gift for a feature writer who wants to make his mark as a knowledgeable person. In fact the more of a specialist he is, the better are the feature writer's chance of selling his product. A feature becomes attractive to editors if it is timely, written by an authority, illustrated suitably. Magazines, especially, prefer features that can be richly illustrated.

Review writing: Review writing is one of the important features of journalism today. Some readers are very interested to read review writing about books, films and dramas. Generally the review of a book is based on the following three parts:

- **First part** contains the title of the book, Author's name, Name of the publisher, Place of availability and its full address, Edition, Price of the book and the Pages of the book.
- **Second part contains** the subject matter of the book; the views of the author on the subject should be clearly given; regarding the views of the author, the review writer may point out the appreciable views and the defects of the book.
- **Third part contains** the views of the review writer, he may give his advice to the author or he may give his recommendations for the readers.
- **Cinema review or film review:** Before release, the films are screened in preview theaters for reviewers and journalists by the producers.

Travelogue: A travelogue is usually a personal account of writer's visit to a city, town which impresses from several aspects like living style, culture, civilization, heritage, prevailing there. Travelogues are also helpful in understanding the people of a place and their pursuits, their philosophy of life and their concerns, their lifestyles, their plans and sorrows. One thing should be clearly understood that these travelogues are usually biased writings of individual writer and whatever they have written is not certainly the real truth about any destination or country.

Editorial writing: The editorial page is considered as one of the attractive features of newspapers. Separate pages are allotted for editorial section in many newspapers. For example 'The Hindu' and 'Indian Express' are having editorial pages.

The contribution that is found in editorial page can be divided into **three types**: They are:

1. Editorial
2. Letters to the Editorial ; and
3. Columns, Articles, Features, Middles etc.

The Editorial page is otherwise called **opinion page in journalism**.

Firstly, the prime problem of the day should be chosen for editorial writing. **Secondly,** the editorial writer has **to collect the materials connected** with the editorial subject.

Thirdly, in the editorial writing **the problem must be introduced in a clearest manner;**

- the history of the problem should be mentioned;
- new problem should be expressed;
- the contrary views regarding this, if any, should be explained clearly;
- the writer may advise the people or the government on that problem.

Finally, a critical analysis of the problem should be given in the editorial writing then only it is considered as a good editorial writing.

Writing and Editing of News

Any news story that appears in a news paper consists on a superficial look of three parts: the headline, the first paragraph usually set in bold and the remainder of the story. The headline is the first to attract the reader. Giving an appropriate headline is an art in itself. Choosing the length and size of the headline is to make the first choice as to its importance and relevance. The headline's message is terse, abrupt and often startling. The whole idea is to make the reader stop and look. The headline seeks to hold attention and compel the reader to read the story.

But an effective headline is not sufficient itself. A great deal depends on the first paragraph. It is called lead because it leads the rest of the story. It is also called the intro because it introduces rest to the reader. If the lead or intro is not sufficiently arresting, interest will lag and the reader's eye may wander on to another headline and another story. Hence importance of writing the catchy first paragraph.

Moving on to **'FIVE W' s and one H**

Five Ws: Convention requires that in the lead the reporter must answer the five W's: Who, What, When, Where, Why and the one H- How? But that was in the old days.

These days it is a convention honoured more in the breach than the observance. In fact a religious observance of the convention would make a lead paragraph unwidely and heavy. The practice nowadays is to write a lead of not more than 30 words. The former International News services style book instructed its staff to write the lead in three lines or less. Any good reporter can tell you that the news can be told effectively within these set limits.

But what exactly is expected of a good lead or intro? The following general points are almost universal:

1. The intro should be **appropriate** for the story.
2. The intro should make the reader want to **read the rest** of the story.
3. The intro should be kept **short** whenever possible.
4. The intro should normally be based on the **key point** of the story.

The next step is to write the story. You have already given the main point of the story in that first paragraph. The remainder of the story should fall into place in a natural sequence. It is as if you have taken the reader by his hand and led him step by step in the finale.

The accepted method of telling the story falls in what is called the "inverted pyramid" pattern. First the intro comes, then facts to back the intro, then possibly a quote, then the background to the intro followed by more facts. The shape of the story would be an inverted pyramid.

A News Story:

A News story has **three parts** they are,

1. The Headline
2. The First Paragraph
3. The Remainder of the Story

***The Headline first attracts us.** It stands out in the bold black type .it tells us quickly what the story covers. Its primary function is to attract our attention.

***The First Paragraph (or) Lead**: It would be difficult to overstate the importance of the lead. Lead remains the primary concern of the newspaper writer. In any form of writing the writer tries to put his best.

Read any modern newspaper today and you will find that by glancing at the headlines and through each lead you will get all the important news. A good lead is required to:

- It **summarizes** the story for the reader.
- It **identifies** the story concerned.

The Inverted pyramid

This refers to the style of journalism which places the most important facts at the beginning and works “down” from there. Ideally, the first paragraph should contain enough information to give the reader a good overview of the story. The rest of article expands and explains the beginning.

In developing the story, the reporter will choose his words carefully, preferring short words for long ones, the familiar word for the unfamiliar one and strong words, for weak ones.

To put together, there are 25 ways in which the newspapers could be published for easier reading. The beginner may not remember all, but they are a good guide to news reporting:

- Use short simple words.
- Use more one-syllable words
- Use familiar words
- Use personal words
- Use concrete words.
- Make every word work
- Avoid technical words
- Get rid of rubber stamp phrases
- Put sparkle and freshness into simple phrases
- Create figures of speech
- Use intimate phrases
- Use short sentences
- Make frequent use of very short sentences
- Use short sentences as an aid to clear thinking
- Makes sentences active
- Use short, simple paragraphs
- Use very short paragraphs for variety and emphasis
- Use one idea paragraphs
- Use paragraphs for action, impact and result
- Write for a specific purpose
- Write to one person, one human being
- Talk to that person write where he is
- Talk to that person in his own field of knowledge
- Work with one basic idea
- Write with one view point

Editing can be defined in so many ways. It includes:

- Preparing a piece of writing for publication: Normally a piece written by another person. Publication may be a book, newspaper or other periodical like magazine.
- Doing the work of planning and directing the publication.

Planning involves the whole work plan like-

1. length or size of the item,
2. nature of item,
3. display of item,
4. time taken in editing,
5. process of editing,
6. arranging tools for editing.

- **Directing involves-**

1. issuing necessary instructions to subordinate staff,
2. monitoring the work assigned to them,
3. interacting with the production staff,
4. controlling the quality of publication.

- **Arranging data for computer processing-related to research/ survey.**

When you have written enough to satisfy the requirements of the assignment or you have said all you ought to say about a given topic, it is time to put your paper through the rewriting process. If you are one of those students who compose on a word processor, you are a step ahead of the game; if not, use the process of going from hand written text to typewritten as one of the steps of rewriting. As you go along, some spell checkers will underline words otherwise alert you with beeps and whistles that words are misspelled or duplicated and you can fix those on the fly. Otherwise, don't bother with spelling here; you can catch misspelling later. But do watch for clumsy phrases in your writing and gaps in your thinking.

FORMATTING: There can be text, abstract, references, tables, figures and legends that should be formatted so that they conform to the journal's instructions.

PROOF READING

Proof reading traditionally means reading a proof copy of a text in order to detect and correct any errors. Modern proof reading often requires reading a copy at earlier stages as well.

A proof is a typeset version of copy or a manuscript page. They often contain typos introduced through human error. Traditionally, a proofreader looks at an increment of text on the copy and then compares it to the corresponding typeset increment, and then marks any errors using standard proofreaders' marks. Unlike copy editing, proofreading's defining procedure is to work directly with two sets of information at the same time.

There are some Alternative methods:

Copy holding or **copy reading** employs two readers per proof. The first reads the text aloud literally as it appears, usually at a comparatively fast but uniform rate. The second reader follows along and marks any pertinent differences between what is read and what was typeset. Mutual understanding is the only guiding principle, so codes evolve as opportunity permits.

Double reading: A single proofreader checks the proof in the traditional manner, but then passes it on to a second reader who repeats the process. Both initial the proof. Note that with both copy holding and double reading, responsibility for a given proof is necessarily shared by two individuals.

Scanning, used to check a proof without reading it word for word, has become common with computerization of typesetting and the popularization of word processing. Before the data in a Word file can be published, it must be converted into a format used by the publisher. The end product is usually called a *conversion*. The publisher is held responsible only for formatting errors, such as typeface, page width, and alignment of columns in tables; and production errors such as text inadvertently deleted. To simplify matters further, a given conversion will usually be assigned a specific template. Given typesetters of sufficient skill, experienced proofreaders familiar with their typesetters' work can accurately scan their pages without reading the text for errors that neither they nor their typesetters are responsible for.

CHAPTER XI

NEWS PHOTOGRAPHY

The term photojournalism was coined in 1940's by Professor Cliff Edom of the University of Missouri. Photography is a personal and fascinating subject. We take pictures to express our feelings about people, nature and the world around us. The purpose of taking photos is to please oneself and to communicate to a small circle of friends and family. Sometimes people take it as a hobby and some others as a profession. Photo journalism is a kind of photography. It deals with people and events. Photojournalism encompasses a broad variety of word and picture reporting.

1. **Get in close**: Photos will often be published on low quality newsprint focus on a single, frame-filling centre of interest not more than two or three people. Not more than a few objects with a clean, contrasting background. If you cannot get in close, crop ruthlessly which destroy the entire image.
2. **Find unusual angles**: Good Photojournalists are always moving to take photographs so that it will cover the whole situation or image.
3. **Get indents:** All subjects easily identifiable must be named. Most editors will reject photos without indents. Ask and write it in your reporter's notebook.
4. **Burn pixels:** Take more number of photos of the situation /function so that it is easy to pick the good pictures.
5. **Avoid obvious posing:** Try to make the scene appear natural. Photojournalism aims to cover people doing things, not people posing.

6. **Add light but don't make it obvious:** Available light is ideal. In some cases, light comes from ugly angles or is so weak you cannot even get close to stopping the action. You need to control

the color balance of bright green florescent or difficult combinations of artificial and natural light. A good Photojournalists carefully analyse the light falling on their subject and find an angle which best enhances the scene.

7. **Go beyond the cliché and over used statement:** Take photographs of unusual scenes look for interesting actions which are not taken by others, but should be eye catching to the public.
8. **Focus faithfully, stay steady:** The photographers should focus properly on the scene to be shot. A blurred photos or many slight fuzziness will be enhanced by poor quality paper and fast reproduction.
9. **Dump poorly exposed photos:** Expose the camera carefully and correctly. Do not use poorly exposed photos for publication.
10. **Have guts:** Photojournalists should be more open minded daring to approach the people to take photographs. Note down their names and should posses a press pass to take close up of sports actions etc.

Basic photojournalism job duties cover much more ground than merely taking photos. In addition to taking news photos, a journalist may be responsible for:

- Brainstorming news ideas with journalists
- Consulting with photo editors
- Developing film
- Editing photos
- Scheduling photo sessions
- Writing the photo caption.

Graphic design is the process of visual communication and problem-solving through the use of typography, space, image and color.

The field is considered a subset of visual communication and communication design, but sometimes the term "graphic design" is used interchangeably with these due to overlapping skills involved. Graphic designers use various methods to create and combine words, symbols, and images to create a visual representation of ideas and messages. A graphic designer may use a combination of typography, visual arts, and page layout techniques to produce a final result. Graphic design often refers to both the process by which the communication is created and the products which are generated.

Common uses of graphic design include identity which is logos and branding, publications, i.e. magazines, newspapers and books, print advertisements, posters, billboards, website graphics and elements, signs and product packaging. For example, a product package might include a logo or other artwork, organized text and pure design elements such as images, shapes and color which unify the piece. Composition is one of the most important features of graphic design, especially when using pre-existing materials or diverse elements.

From road signs to technical schematics, from interoffice memorandums to reference manuals, graphic design enhances transfer of knowledge and visual messages. Readability and legibility is enhanced by improving the visual presentation and layout of text.

Design can also aid in selling a product or idea through effective visual communication. It is applied to products and elements of company identity like logos, colors, packaging, and text. Branding has increasingly become important in the range of services offered by many graphic designers, alongside corporate identity. Graphic designers will often form part of a team working on corporate identity and branding projects. Other members of that team can include marketing professionals, communications consultants and commercial writers. It is also applied to layout and formatting of educational material to make the information more accessible and more readily understandable.

Graphic way finding signage systems have become important for large public spaces such as airports and convention centers.

These systems often depend on graphic design to communicate information quickly and economically through a color or symbol that can be read and followed from a distance. Such environmental graphic design systems allow people to navigate unfamiliar spaces.

Graphic design is applied in the entertainment industry in decoration, scenery, and visual story telling. Other examples of design for entertainment purposes include novels, comic books, DVD covers, opening credits and closing credits in filmmaking, and programs and props on stage. This could also include artwork used for T-shirts and other items screen printed for sale.

From scientific journals to news reporting, the presentation of opinion and facts is often improved with graphics and thoughtful compositions of visual information - known as information design. Newspapers, magazines, blogs, television and film documentaries may use graphic design to inform and entertain. With the advent of the web, information designers with experience in interactive tools such as Adobe Flash are increasingly being used to illustrate the background to news stories.

METHODS OF PRINTING

A printing process describes the method adopted by a system to transfer the image on to a substrate or material. This also means that a printing system will have a medium that carries the image in the first place before it enables the process of reproduction. Getting this printing surface prepared is dependent on the printing process. Over the years, many different ways of putting ink on paper developed and these evolved to be the printing processes. The mechanics adopted under different systems are so different that they cater to specific applications in the market.

The first ever press was a **Letterpress**. It basically uses stamps to grab ink and place it on the paper or other material. Think of a typewriter, but doing whole pages in one press. Of course, this took long to do as each page was setup before by hand and manually placing these letter stamps in place. As time went on, full page stamps were created instead to make the process easier. Today however, the Letterpress is not used much as it is not an efficient and far too expensive method of printing.

Offset Lithography

This method of printing is the most common and oldest used today. It works on the principle that water and oil which is ink don't mix. Using metal or polyester sheets called plates, image and non-image areas are burned onto the plate using light to expose the image areas. This plate is attached onto a cylinder that as it goes around on the press, picks up water onto the non image areas. since water and oil don't mix, when the plate comes into contact with the ink, it only sticks to where the water isn't, our image area. The plate then comes into contact with a rubber sheet called a blanket and it transfers the image. The blanket them rotates around and presses to image into the paper. This is where the offset term comes from. While other methods can be done with offset theories, the Offset Lithography is so common that when someone refers to offset printing, this is what they mean.

Flexography

This is traditionally used to print labels. If you look at a bottle of PoP, the plastic or cellophane label on it was likely done by flexography. It is the packaging industry who primarily uses flexography. The idea behind flexography is similar to a Letterpress where it uses a stamp, but this one is created with rubber etched with tiny grooves that pick up ink. The rubber stamp or plate wrapped around a cylinder which rotates and picks up ink from a reservoir then presses it into the printing material. This is often done on plastics, tissues, labels, stickers and cardboard.

Gravure

This is a method usually used in printing long runs of magazines. Much like flexography, gravure printing has a cylinder that picks up ink in tiny etched grooves and places it on the paper. The difference is, gravure doesn't use a plate. Its grooves are actually etched into the cylinder. This allows it to last much longer and can be used for more impressions before it wears out.

Screen Printing

This is still a common method of printing. It is often used on all the odd materials. Solid letters on plastics, T-shirts and clothing materials, a lot of signs and others use screen printing. The idea behind screen prints is basically a screened material such as silk or nylon is stretched across a frame and fastened into place. A stencil, cut by hand or made electronically, is placed over that screen to block out on non printing areas. Ink is placed inside the frame and scrapped across the stencil with a rubber squeegee. The ink goes through the screen and onto the material.

Digital Printing

There are several ways to do digital printing. Many methods try to reproduce the effects of the previously described styles. There are inkjet, laser and toner, and magnetic digital printers. In inkjet, the ink cartridge holds liquid ink that is released in tiny sprays onto the paper. It makes several dots, that when viewed without a magnifying glass creates the illusion of your image. Laser and toner method uses a laser to charge the paper in certain areas which will attract toner of CYMK colours to it. It then goes through a fuser which melts the toner into the paper. Magnetic works in much the same way but instead of electrical charges, it uses magnetic ones. It also passes through a fuser to melt the toner on.

This is all just touching the tip of the iceberg for each of these methods. This is just a rough summary of what these printing methods are all about. If you are interested in learning more, the internet has all the information you could want about this. Printing is considered the greatest invention of the second millennium and is a major reason why we are where we are today.

Ethics of News photography

There are several miscellaneous issues that photojournalists regularly face that do not fit into the neat and ordered categories of victims of violence, rights to privacy, and picture manipulations. Nevertheless, when a photographer is confronted with one of them, the ethical problems the issues pose can be equally troubling for photographers and editors.

Some tips are based on commonly accepted editorial values adopted by most mainstream media.

Accuracy

- Keep an accurate record of all you shoot including time, date, location, circumstances and details of all the parties involved in the event you are covering.
- The research for the story behind the images you are shooting should be well- sourced, supported by strong evidence, examined and tested, clear and unambiguous.
- Don't just go for the shocking, sad and emotionally charged images; to do so might exploit the victims and fail to uncover the cause of the distress.
- Never accept what you are told at face value; always check every detail with two independent sources.
- Always be aware that there will be those who will want to set up an event for their own purposes; be wary if you are offered an amazing photo opportunity.
- Be sure that what you photograph reflects the true situation accurately and is not a distortion of reality; on the other hand, never ignore the one-off that could reveal an aspect of neglect or harm that has so far gone unnoticed.
- You don't need to have the whole story behind what you see, but you do need to be totally open, honest and transparent about what you know and what you don't know.
- Never follow the pack; they may be being led and fed by those with ulterior motives.
- Build your own trusted contacts so that you are able to distinguish between fact and spin.
- Be careful when filming an incident or a subject when you are not culturally familiar with the background and circumstances; what may seem shocking to you may only reflect one element of a complex story.
- Don't crop or edit beyond what is technically necessary to display the image; you could distort more than the picture – you

will know instinctively when you have crossed the line between editing and manipulation.

- Never stage-manage a shoot to hype up the story; your job is to report through images what has actually happened.
- Don't just go for the shocking, sad and emotionally charged images; to do so might exploit the victims and fail to uncover the cause of the distress.

Impartiality

- Be careful when filming topics about which you are passionately concerned; you could lose your objectivity and do more harm than good.
- If you have an interest in covering an event, make that absolutely clear in the text that accompanies your work.
- Aim to offer all sides of the story in context and in a way that enables the audience to reach a reasoned and informed conclusion.
- Your only motivation should be to inform the public debate and shine a light on wrong doing and abuse.
- Being impartial and objective means not being prejudiced but being fair and balanced; be sure to recognize when you are getting carried away.
- Always rise above your own personal perspective and try to see a story from other points of view; otherwise your work is likely to be one sided and limited in scope value.
- Ensure that you reflect a wide range of opinions through your camera lens, and be prepared to explore conflicting views so that no significant point of view is left out.
- Be careful when filming topics about which you are passionately concerned; you could lose your objectivity and do more harm than good.

Taste & decency and offence

- Do not be afraid of offending if the information you are covering is in the public interest.
- Avoid gratuitous imagery that shocks rather than enhances the understanding of the audience; you are not there to sensationalise or impress.
- Do not be afraid of offending if the information you are covering is in the public interest.

Privacy and consent

- Respect a person's privacy, especially the vulnerable; their situation should not be seen as a rung on your career ladder.
- Ensure that those you are filming are aware of how and where the images are going to be used. If they are to be used online as well as in print or broadcast ensure that those being filmed understand that the images will be searchable forever.
- Respect a person's privacy, especially the vulnerable; their situation should not be seen as a rung on your career ladder.

Integrity

- Never expose someone to ridicule and humiliation; they have to live with the fallout the photograph will bring, whereas you may have moved on to the next story and suffer no consequences.
- Always remember you are working as a video/photo journalist to inform the public debate, not for your own glory or to try to make yourself look good.
- Never expose a subject to danger in order to improve the shot; take what is natural, warts and all.
- Never take payment, promises or favours in return for covering an event in a certain way or submitting a photograph that serves a cause.
- Never expose a subject to danger in order to improve the shot; take what is natural, warts and all.

Since a picture or visual presentation of news creates a stronger and more lasting impression on the readers and viewers than mere words, photojournalists and other visual news producers have to be a lot more responsible and careful in the discharge of their duties. They must, therefore, ensure that in keeping with the high standards of journalism, their presentations are always in public interest, fair, accurate, unbiased, sober and decent.

Adherence to the following do's and don'ts will surely help them self-regulate their conduct and maintain their professional integrity and high standards:

DO'S

1. Images should be accurate and comprehensive and the subjects be presented in proper context.
2. All subjects should be treated with respect and dignity. Special consideration is given to vulnerable subjects and victims of crime or tragedy be treated compassionately. Private grief is intruded only when the public has an overriding and justifiable interest in sharing or viewing it.
3. While editing a visual, the maintenance of the integrity of the content and context of the photographic images should be ensured. Images should not be manipulated neither should there be addition or alteration in sound in any way that can mislead viewers or misrepresent subjects.
4. Strive to be unobtrusive and humble in dealing with subjects.
5. The integrity of the photographic moment should be respected.
6. Pictures should not reflect anything that is obscene, vulgar or offensive to good public taste.
7. Strive to ensure that the public's business is conducted in public. Defend the rights of access for all journalists.
8. Strive for total and unrestricted access to subjects and recommend alternatives to shallow or rushed opportunities.
9. Seek a diversity of viewpoints and work to show unpopular or unnoticed points of view.

10. Strive by example and influence to maintain the spirit and high standards expressed in this code.
11. When confronted with situations in which proper action is not clear, seek the counsel of those who exhibit the highest standards of the profession.

Now we move on to the DON'TS

1. A newspaper proposing to report a sting operation shall obtain a certificate from the person who recorded or produced the same certifying that the operation is genuine and bonafide.
2. There must be concurrent record in writing of the various stages of the sting operation.
3. Decision to report the sting operation should be taken by the editor after satisfying himself of the public interest of the matter and ensuring that report complies with all legal requirements.
4. Sting operation published in print media should be scheduled with the awareness of the likely reader in mind. Great care and sensitivity should be exercised to avoid shocking or offending the reader.
5. While photographing subjects do not intentionally contribute to, alter, or seek to alter or influence events.
6. The privacy of an individual should not be intruded or invaded unless it is outweighed by genuine overriding public interest, not by a prurient or morbid curiosity.
7. While covering terrorist attacks, communal riots or other acts of violence, do not show mangled corpses or such other images as cause revulsion or terror.
8. Do not get manipulated by staged photo opportunities.
9. Do not accept gifts, favours or compensation from those who might seek to influence the coverage.
10. Avoid political, civic or business involvements or employment that could compromise or appear to compromise their professional independence.

11. No payment or material reward should be made to the sources or subject for information or participation.
13. The work should not reflect any kind of biases.
14. Do not intentionally sabotage the efforts of other journalists.

The use of photography as a way of reporting news did not become widespread until the advent of smaller, more portable cameras that used an enlargeable film negative to record images. The introduction of the 35 mm Leica camera in 1925 made it possible for photographers to move with the action, take multiple shots of events as they were unfolding, as well as be more able to create a narrative through their photographs alone.

Since the 1960s, motor drives, electronic flash, auto-focus, better lenses and other camera enhancements have made picture-taking easier. New digital cameras free photojournalists from the limitation of film roll length. Although the number depends on the amount of megapixels the camera contains, whether one's shooting mode is JPEG or RAW, and what size of memory card one is using, it is possible to store thousands of images on a single memory card.

There is some concern by news photographers that the profession of photojournalism as it is known today could change to such a degree that it is unrecognizable as image- capturing technology naturally progresses. Citizen journalism and the increase in user contribution and submission of amateur photos to news sites are becoming increasingly widespread.

Citizen journalism has become more popular with the development and availability of more powerful cameras and equipment. This makes each individual who owns a camera or camera phone aware of their own surroundings, capturing the moment and publishing them online. Photographs are a testament to what has happened in the past and present, capable of making people aware of events and situations which are happening in other places.

CHAPTER XII

ETHICS AND LEGAL ISSUES IN PRINT MEDIA

Media should act as watchdog for the society and so they have a right to cover anything that is new dimension in the society or that has an impact on the society. The explosion of investments in the area of news is the main reason for the news people getting into marketing mode rather than stay in the mode of being watchdogs and communicators to the society. These conditions led the focus towards business ahead of journalist's ethic. The judgment now is if something is news worthy. The matter of concern now is, should media cover those potentially dangerous aspects of the society at prime time to protect the interest of a very small section of population even if such a story impacts the larger section of the society adversely. The term 'unethical' is used in connection with media either to mean prohibited or not allowable.

The press council of India has been established with the object **of preserving the freedom of the press and of maintaining and improving the standards of newspaper and news agencies** in the country. The council over the years has built up a code of ethics covering aspects of journalism.

The ethics are not imposed on the profession from outside, but are evolved by itself. The fundamental duty and responsibility enjoins on the profession many other moral and ethical obligations, like:

- Need to verify from all possible sources the correctness of their stories, particularly libelous and defamatory material, before publication.
- Need to exercise utmost caution in reporting communal disturbances, scrupulously avoiding inflammatory material.

- While publishing "letters to the editor" or covering proceeding of parliament duty to give a balanced picture, taking views of all sides involved; and
- Not to publish unverified, baseless, graceless, misleading or distorted material
- Not to condemn anyone unheard
- Not to invade a person's privacy, except in clear public interest
- Not to steal another person's writing, that is use another authors writing as your own;
- Not to criticize the judicial acts of a judge adversely affecting the administration of justice

The ethical guidelines prescribed for the print media are not exhaustive but only selective to bring home. The fact that the purpose of codifying the ethico- moral principles is to make the press fully responsible to the society as a whole and to be fair to individuals, so that the print media functions in the best interest of the people.

Code of Ethics for the Press in Reporting and Commenting on Communal Incidents Adopted in 1968 at All India Newspaper Editors' Conference.

1. A free press can flourish only in a free society. Communalism is a threat to the fabric of our free society and to the nation's solidarity.
2. The press has a vital role to play in the consummation of the fundamental objectives enshrined in our Constitution, namely, democracy, secularism, national unity, and integrity and the rule of law. It is the duty of the press to help promote unity and cohesion in the hearts and minds of the people, and refrain from publishing material tending to excite communal passions or inflame communal hatred.
3. To this end the press should adhere to the following guidelines in reporting on communal incidents in the country:

- All editorial comments and other expressions of opinion, whether through articles, letters to the Editor, or in any other form should be restrained and free from scurrilous attacks against leaders or communities, and there should be no incitement to violence.

Besides these wire agencies, a large number of agencies which deliver news material and articles by hand or mail, like the old established India Press agency, INFA (India News and Feature Alliance), and Press Asia International, and several agencies in Delhi and outside, some, as we will see, in Hindi, Urdu and other languages. There are also photo agencies and a cartographic service. Photo journalism as well as cartoons has developed fast and a news paper can hardly afford to go without either. There are also agencies in the electronic field for the benefit of subscribers at home and abroad. Amongst all these news agencies, PTI and UNI have made a great impact in the distribution of national and international news in India.

There are also Press organizations that control the press regarding the news that will be published.

Audit bureau of circulation Ltd. (ABC): the ABC is a private body whose members are 252 regional and national publishers and 208 leading advertisers, news agencies and advertising agencies. It surveys the circulation of publications in English, Hindi and 12 regional languages, in more than 80 major Indian towns. It carries out circulation surveys on regular basis and issues certificates of Net Paid Circulation, every six months. It has a very high reputation for reliability and impartiality. Therefore, it is quoted with authority.

Another press organization is Registrar of Newspapers for India (RNI): RNI functions as Central Government body responsible for the compilation of a register giving particulars like ownership and circulation of all newspapers published in India. It overseas the allocation of titles, news print, and certificates for the impart of printing and allied machinery required by newspaper establishments. It also sees to the enforcement of the provision of the Press and Regulation of Books Act, and has the authority to inspect newspapers records and documents. It carries out frequent checks to find out whether the newspapers registered with it are published regularly and also whether the circulation figures claimed by newspapers are credible. It complies the Annual Report of the Press in India.

The Press Information Bureau (PIB): PIB is the central agency of the government of India. It disseminates information on government policies, decisions, programmes, initiatives and activities. It puts out this information to daily newspapers, periodicals, news agencies and All India Radio and Doordarshan. It provides feedback to the concerned ministry or department of the government of India regarding press relations and nature and extent of publicity measures to be adopted. It accordingly advises the Government of India on its information policy.

According to the Constitution of India, there are various Laws that govern the print media.

They are

- Press Council of India
- Constitutional law of Press freedom
- Press and Registration of books
- Official Secrets Act
- Contempt of Courts
- Privileges of Parliament
- Working Journalist's Act
- Copyright Act
- Law of Defamation

CONSTITUTIONAL LAW OF PRESS FREEDOM

India is one of those countries which guarantee their citizens the right to freely express themselves. The Indian Constitution guarantees fundamental freedoms, and the 'freedom of speech and expression' is the first among them.

Article 19(1) of the constitution reads: all citizens shall have the right to:

a. Freedom of speech and expression;
b. Assemble peacefully and without arms;
c. Form associations and millions;
d. Move freely throughout the territory of India;
e. Reside and settle in any part of the territory of India;
f. Practice any profession of to carryon any occupation, trade or business.

Thus all Indian citizens enjoy a constitutional right & give free expression to their views, opinions, and convictions. They have for this, purpose, the right to seek.

PRESS COUNCIL OF INDIA ACT, 1978

The PCI is also to promote a proper functional relationship among all classes of persons in news-papers and news agencies, concern itself with developments such as concentration of ownership affecting independence of the press and take up any other studies related to the press that may be referred to it by the Centre. The objective of the PCI is to preserve the freedom of the press and to improve the standards and maintain their independence, build up a code of conduct for them in accordance with high professional standards, ensure maintenance of received by Indian newspapers and agencies from any foreign sources as referred to it by the Centre. The Centre can, at the same time, deal with such cases in any other manner it thinks fit. The Council may be entrusted with a study of the impact and circulation of foreign newspapers and their correspondents. The newspapers may include embassy publications.

PRESS AND REGISTRATION OF BOOKS ACT

The oldest surviving Act in this regard is the Press and Registration of Books Act, 1867. It also remained the fundamental law governing the rules for the regulation of the publication of newspapers and of having printing presses. The Act requires that the name of the printer, the place of printing and the name of the publisher and place of publication must be legibly printed on every book or newspaper printed/published within India .

For having a press to print books or newspapers, a declaration must be made before the District Presidency or Sub-divisional Magistrate giving description of its location.

Two conditions are necessary to be fulfilled for publishing a newspaper.

1. The name of the editor must be clearly printed on every copy of the newspaper.
2. A declaration must be made before the District, Presidency or Sub-divisional Magistrate within whose jurisdiction the newspaper is to be published, stating the facts:

    a. Name *of* the printer and publisher

    b. Premises where printing and publishing is conducted,
    c. The title, language and periodicity of the newspaper.

The declaration should be made by the printer and publisher either in person or through an authorized agent. If the printer or publisher is not the owner of the paper, the declaration should specify the 'name of the owner. But, making a declaration does not automatically pave the way for publishing a newspaper. Publication can be started only after the said Magistrate authenticates the declaration.

OFFICIAL SECRETS ACT

The Official Secrets Act, 1923 is a comprehensive document relating to official secrets and defines a number of offences. The Act is aimed at maintaining the security of the State against leakage of secret information, sabotage and the like. However, many of the acts prohibited by this law may be committed by newspapers and journalists, as private individuals, while performing their duties.

The Official Secret Act, 1923 broadly has two parts-one relating to spying for the enemies. The punishment for spying in relation to the country's defence is upto fourteen years. The other relates to unauthorized communication of any other secret official code or passwords or any sketch, plan, model, article, note, document or information .

The provision of Sec.5 is more important from the stand-point of the freedom of the press. The Government whose administrative culture is secrecy, has an internal system of dividing its documents into 'classified' and 'non-classified' categories. The classified documents are considered secret under various statues, such as "Top Secret", "Secret", "Confidential" and "Restricted personal–note for publication". Laws against printing of classified documents are understandable in relation to certain areas like defence and security of the country. But, the Official Secret Act also prohibits publication or communication of any information, which may be directly or indirectly useful to the enemy.

In India it has been widely demanded that Section 5 of the Official Secrets Act which inhibits free reporting should be done away with. It prescribes a punishment with imprisonment upto five years or fine or with both for a person who voluntarily receives or communicates any official secret. The Act does so without defining an official secrete. This means that any official information which has been deemed by the authorities as secret can be published only on the pain of punishment.

CONTEMPT OF COURTS

Judiciary is the most important of the three pillars of the government. It interprets laws. The judiciary settles disputes between individuals, between the individual and the State, and among the various constituents of the State. In order that it is effective all must have faith and confidence in its impartiality, fairness and concern for the rights of the individual, interest of the State and the good of the society. For this its independence must be ensured. There must be no interference in its functioning and no attempt to intimidate or influence it. Any such thing shall be done on the pain of punishment.

According to Sec. 2 of the Contempt of Courts Act, 1971, contempt is of two kinds '-

- Civil Contempt and Criminal Contempt: Civil contempt means willful disobedience to any judgment, decree, direction, order writ or other process of a court, **or willful** breach of an undertaking given to a court
- Criminal contempt means publication of any matter or doing of any other act whatsoever , which
- Scandalizes or tends to scandalize or lowers or tends to lower the authority of any court or
- Prejudices or interferes or tends to interfere with the due course of any judicial proceeding; or
- Interferes or tends to interfere or obstructs or tends to obstruct the administration of justice in any

  other manner.

- Scandalisation here means scurrilous attack on the administration of justice or vilification of the entire judiciary, a particular judge or a particular court.

PRIVILEGES OF PARLIAMENT

The concept of privileges of Parliament rests on the principle that a sovereign legislature should be able to perform its legislative and deliberative functions independently and effectively. For this it should possess certain inherent or conferred powers to punish for breach of such privileges.

Articles 105 (3) and 194 (3) of the Constitution empower Parliament and State Legislatures respectively to enact laws codifying their privileges. However, neither Parliament nor any of the legislatures of the States has so far done so. Therefore, according to the Constitution itself, the privileges enjoyed by them are the same as, and not more than, those of the British House of Commons. One has to wade through the rulings, customs and practices of the House of Commons and to seek guidance for the Rules of Business and Conduct Proceedings of the House. Breach of privilege of either House of central or state legislature is usually known as 'contempt of Parliament' like the contempt of courts.

WORKING JOURNALISTS ACT

The Working Journalists and other Newspaper Employees and Miscellaneous Provisions Act, 1955 is a welfare measure meant to regulate conditions of service of the people employed in the newspaper industry.

It is related mainly to

- Special provisions in respect of certain cases of retrenchment
- Payment of gratuity
- Hours of work
- Leave
- Fixation of revision of rates of wages
- Enforcement of the recommendations of the wage fixation machinery i.e., wage boards and wage tribunals
- Employee's Provident fund
- Recovery of money due from the employer

In order to fix or revise rates of wages, separate Wage Boards for working journalists and other newspaper employees can be set up under the Act. The wage Board for journalists consist of a chairman, two representing working journalists and two independent persons. In the Wage Board for non-journalist newspaper employees, two persons representing them shall be included. The chairman of both the Boards is to be an independent person who is or has been a Judge of the High Court or the Supreme Court.

The Central Government may fix interim rates of wages in consultation with the Boards.

Money due to an employee under this Act can be recovered from the employer by the Collector in the same manner as an arrear of land revenue, and have it paid to the employee.

COPY RIGHT ACT, 1957

A work of literature, drama, music or art is an intellectual property. It must be protected from illegal copying or reproducing it. The Copyright Act, 1957 accords this protection. The law is based on two competing considerations.

1. The creator's property, that is, the original works need to be protected.
2. For advancement of knowledge in the interest of the society, there should be some amount of freedom to produce parts of other people's copyrighted works.

Copyright has been held to be a right which a person acquires in a work which is the result of his intellectual labour. The primary function of the copyright law is to protect from annexation by other people the fruits of a man's work, labour or skill.

In respect of the Press, copyright means, under Section14 of the Copyright Act, 1957, the exclusive right in the case of a literary, dramatic and musical work, to do and authorize the doing in substantive form of any of the following acts, namely:

i. to reproduce the work in any material form;
ii. to publish the work;
iii. to make any adoption of a work; and
iv. to reproduce or publish translation of the work.

Punishment for knowingly infringing or abetting the infringement of a copy right is imprisonment which may exceed up to one year or fine or both.

Now we will discuss about Law of Defamation. The background of law of defamation is:

Defamation or taking away the fame from someone is an offence punishable with imprisonment from the earliest times of civil government. There is no separate law of defamation in India. The Indian Penal Code (IPC) has four sections which define elaborately what constitutes defamation and what the defenses and the punishments are. Defamation is of two kinds:

1. Verbal defamation is known as slander
2. Written defamation is termed as libel.

The ingredients of the offence of defamation are:

i. An imputation concerning the person must have been made.
ii. Such imputation must have harmed, or there is reason to believe that it has the tendency to harm, the reputation of the person concerning whom it is made.

Imputation means an accusation against a person and implies an allegation of fact and not merely a term of abuse or insult. In order to constitute the offence of defamation, it is not necessary that an injury to the reputation of the complainant must have been actually caused. It is enough if the offending statement is made with the intention of harming the reputation of the complainant or with knowledge or reason to believe that it will harm his reputation.

1. A false and defamatory statement concerning another;
2. The unprivileged publication of the statement to a third party
3. If the defamatory matter is of public concern, fault amounting at least to negligence on the part of the publisher; and
4. Damage to the plaintiff.

In the context of defamation law, a statement is "published" when it is made to the third party. That term does not mean that the statement has to be in print.

Damages are typically to the reputation of the plaintiff, but depending upon the laws of the jurisdiction it may be enough to establish mental anguish.

Most jurisdictions also recognize "per se" defamation, where the allegations are presumed to cause damage to the plaintiff.

- Attacks on a person's professional character or standing;
- Allegations that an unmarried person is unchaste;
- Allegations that a person is infected with a sexually transmitted disease;
- Allegations that the person has committed a crime of moral turpitude;

While actions for defamation have their roots in common law, most jurisdictions have now enacted statutes which modify the common law. They may change the elements of the cause of action, limit when an action may be filed, or modify the defenses to an action for defamation. Some may even require that the defendant be given an opportunity to apologize before the plaintiff can seek non-economic damages.

Punishment for defamation

Section 500 IPC prescribes the punishment for defamation.

"Whoever defames another shall be punished with simple imprisonment for a term which may extend to two years, or with fine, or with both".

Section 501 of IPC makes "printing or engraving matter known to be defamatory" and section 502 makes "sale of printed or engraved substance containing defamatory matter" also offences punishable with simple imprisonment which may extend to two years, or with fine, or both.

The Press Council of India has been established with the objects of preserving the freedom of the Press and of maintaining, improving the standards of newspapers and news agencies in the country.

It is to further these objects, that the Council is required among other things,

1. to help newspapers and news agencies to maintain independence;
2. to build up a code of conduct for newspapers agencies and journalists in accordance with high professional stands to ensure on their parts the maintenance of high standards of public taste and to foster a due sense of the rights and responsibilities of citizenship and to foster the growth of a sense of responsibility and public service among all those engaged in the profession of journalism.

CHAPTER XIII

ELECTRONIC MEDIA

Electronic media are media that utilize electronics or electromechanical energy for the end user, i.e. the audience to access the content.

This is in contrast to static media, mainly print media, which are more often created electronically, but don't require electronics to be accessed by the end user in the printed form.

Communication media like television, radio, audio, video etc. has made possible news, entertainment, information, education related subjects reach the very far and wide places. It has to an extent sidelined other forms of communication. With the growing network of TV, satellite communication, cable services, radio stations, etc., the future of this industry seems bright.

The primary electronic media sources familiar to the general public are better known as video recordings, audio recordings, multimedia presentations, slide presentations, CD- ROM and Online Content. Most new media are in the form of digital media. However, electronic media may be in either analog or digital format.

Advancements in digital technologies have dramatically altered the practice of journalism. Satellite and Video-phones, the internet, digital audio recorders and laptop computers allow instantaneous communication between most destinations in the world. The outcome is electronic journalism - a convergence of new media technologies, ultimately resulting in a change in the manner in which journalists of the twenty-first century deliver the news. The news environment has been significantly altered by electronic journalism, as news organizations now have the ability to gather, produce and transmit information readily and instantaneously to the public. Digital advancements have proved the immediacy of news, as journalists are able to broadcast live from any destination and are able to send messages or images and video footage directly to newsrooms, via video-phones.

Although the term is usually associated with the content recorded on a storage medium, recordings are not required for live broadcasting and online networking.

Television and radio programs are distributed through radio broadcasting or cable or often both simultaneously. By coding signals and having decoding equipment in homes, the latter also enables subscription-based channels and pay-per-view services. Broadcasting forms a very large segment of the mass media. A broadcasting organization may broadcast several programs at the same time, through several channels or frequencies, for example like BBC One and Two, Discovery channel and National Geographic, etc. On the other hand, two or more organizations may share a channel and each use it during a fixed part of the day.

Digital radio and digital television may also transmit multiplexed programming, with several channels compressed into one ensemble. When Broadcasting to a very narrow range of audience, it is called narrowcasting. Contrary to some common usage, the Internet and the World Wide Web are not synonymous. The Internet is a collection of interconnected computer networks, linked by copper wires, fiber-optic cables, wireless connections etc. The intervention of the Internet has also allowed breaking news stories to reach around the globe within minutes.

There is also Web, which is a collection of interconnected documents, linked by hyperlinks and URLs. The World Wide Web is accessible via the Internet, along with many other services including e-mail, file sharing with anyone with a web site can address a global audience.

Prasar Bharathi

Prasar Bharati is India's largest public broadcasting organisation. It is an autonomous body set up by an Act of Parliament and comprises of Doordarshan Television Network and All India Radio which were earlier media units of the Ministry of Information and Broadcasting. The Act received assent from President of India on 12

September 1990 after being unanimously passed by Parliament and was finally implemented in November 1997.

The Prasar Bharati Act provides for establishment of a Broadcasting Corporation, to be known as Prasar Bharati, to define its composition, functions and powers. The Act grants autonomy to All India Radio and Doordarshan, which were previously under government control. By the Prasar Bharati Act, all the property, assets, debts, liabilities, payments of money due, all suits and legal proceedings involving Akashvani and Doordarshan were transferred to Prasar Bharati.

Coming to the aspect of autonomous organization. As an organization the Prasar Bharati Board stipulates the act general superintendence, direction and management of affairs of the Corporation vests in Prasar Bharati Board only, which may exercise all such powers and do all such acts and things as may be exercised and done by the Corporation.

In Prasar Bharati Board, there will be:

- A Chairman
- One Executive Member
- One Member (Finance)
- One Member (Personnel)
- Six Part-time Members
- Director-General (Akashvani), *ex officio*
- Director-General (Doordarshan), *ex officio*
- There will also be One representative of the Union Ministry of Information and Broadcasting (i.e. Indian Ministry), to be nominated by that Ministry also and
- There will be two representatives of the employees of the Corporation also, of whom one shall be elected by the engineering staff from amongst the staff and one shall be elected by the other employee from amongst themselves.

The President of India appoints Chairman and the other Members, except the *ex officio* members, nominated member and the elected members.

The Board shall meet not be less than six meetings every year but three months shall not intervene between one meeting and the next meeting.

Let us learn about the **Functions and Objectives** of the Board: The primary duty of this Corporation is to organise and conduct public broadcasting services to inform, educate and entertain the public and to ensure a balanced development of broadcasting on radio and television. The Corporation shall, in the discharge of its functions, be guided by the following objectives, namely:

- Upholding the unity and integrity of the country and the values enshrined in the Constitution.
- Safeguarding the citizen's right to be informed freely, truthfully and objectively on all matters of public interest, national or international, and presenting a fair and balanced flow of information including contrasting views without advocating any opinion or ideology of its own.
- Paying special attention to the fields of education and spread of literacy, agriculture, rural development, environment, health and family welfare and science and technology also.
- Providing adequate coverage to the diverse cultures and languages of the various regions of the country by broadcasting appropriate programmes.
- Also providing adequate coverage to sports and games so as to encourage healthy competition and the spirit of sportsmanship also.
- Providing appropriate programmes keeping in view the special needs of the youth.
- Informing and stimulating the national consciousness in regard to the status and problems of women and paying special attention to the upliftment of women.
- Promoting social justice and combating exploitation, inequality and such evils as untouchability and advancing the welfare of the weaker sections of the society.

- Safeguarding the rights of the working classes and advancing their welfare.
- Serving the rural and weaker sections of the people and those residing in border regions, backward and remote areas.
- Providing suitable programmes keeping in view the special needs of the minorities and tribal communities.
- Taking special steps to protect the interests of children, the blind, the aged, the handicapped and other vulnerable sections of the people.
- Promoting national integration by broadcasting in a manner that facilitates communication in the languages in India; and facilitating the distribution of regional broadcasting services in every State in the languages of that State.

Ethics and Media policies for electronic Media

The term 'unethical' is used in connection with electronic media either to mean prohibited or not allowable. To equate 'ethical' with 'acceptable' and think referring to codes of ethics as 'Acceptable Use Policies' is necessary for electronic media to be up to standard in the public eye.

The explosion of investments in the area of news is the main reason for the news people getting into marketing mode rather than stay in the mode of being watchdogs and communicators to the society. You need to be creative about what you show or write and those stories also should have some spicy content so that they can inspire people easily.

It is important for the media to present anomalous issues taking place in the society to make the people aware of the issues. Members of public will use their judgment while using the information they receive from the media.

But there is unfairness even in presentation of news. One topic may be a good news item and society needs to know the new things happening around. But the way such a topic is presented can be harmful as well.

However, if media presentation is optioned instead of reporting of occurring of an event, it can impact the public opinion. All members of the public are not matured enough to handle the explosive information they receive from the media. We have kids, growing adolescents, and youth, oppressed women who could not get good education or worldview.

While dealing with shaping of public behavior media, we need to be careful to communicate the point as a news item rather than as an opinion. Topics with positive tone were not getting realistic attention. In addition, spicy titles leading to misunderstanding of the topic communicated should be avoided. There are some principles to be remembered while presenting the news as media should realize the responsibility vested on it by the society and impact it can have on the society. To play the respected role media gets in the public eye a set of ethical code that should be used.

THE PRINCIPLES ARE:

1. Judge the news based on the impact it may have on the society. If the positive impact is more than negative the topic is news worthy.
2. Make sure that the sensitive topics are presented without interpretations and opinions. That will help public understand an event or behavior pattern and use their produce to judge.
3. Do not show those things that can have disturbing impact on the society. Showing dead bodies in the TV closely or writing the modus operandi of a social ill such as adultery or prostitution etc should be not in direct terms but merely indicative.
4. Be sensitive to the demographic of the viewers or readers. Do not carry objectionable topics at prime times, which can attract the attention of the young who cannot make judgments about the information they receive.
5. Try to focus on research to find out what positive topics sell like negative topics. It is easy to impact the basic instincts and sell but it may be a popular practice to alert viewers about public crowding or impact of wrong driving habits.

6. *Principle six is o*ur journalists need prudence or maturity. Just use journalist's brain more than the marketer's brain.

And next generations will be deprived of such education and they have an intuition warning them about the immoral behavior while covering a topic and making it news.

Investigative journalism is not born with TV news channels and there were incidents that led to large-scale reform of social and legal structures after exposure of some social practices that are detrimental to the larger interests of the society.

Invading privacy to expose specific issues is prima facie wrong because the behavior of the people involved in the expose is not natural. They are motivated to commit a crime or present misdemeanor and that is being showed as a crime.

Let us learn what are different **Legal and Ethical Issues** that are present for major issues in video production, especially broadcast television. First and foremost let us list on what they are? They are

- Sting Operations
- Invasion of privacy
- Libel
- Slander

- Copyright
- Rights

1. **Sting Operations:** In law enforcement, a sting operation is a deceptive operation designed to catch a person committing a crime. A typical sting will have a law- enforcement officer or cooperative member of the public play a role as criminal partner or potential victim and go along with a suspect's actions to gather evidence of the suspect's wrongdoing.
2. **Privacy for Public and Private Individuals:** Any person needs a space or solitude for himself. The constitution does not talk about a right of privacy or invasion of privacy. But, throughout

the years courts have held that citizens need protection from the unwarranted or unjustified publication of images and information of a private nature.

3. **Then comes the Intrusion / Invasion:** One type of invasion of privacy is intrusion, also referred to as intrusion on selection, or intrusion on solitude. Over hearing and publicizing private conversations or broadcasting images taken from private property typically constitutes an invasion of privacy. Journalists often record audio in-person interviews and telephonic conversations. Although asking permission to records an interview may immediate some people, it makes it possible for you to double check quotes and its cheap insurance in case the person later claims that he or she was misquoted.
4. **Next comes the Access:** News people may decide to go onto private property in the pursuit of information or pictures- until they are specifically asked to leave. Once you move to private property, you need permission either from the owner of the property or his "agent", i.e. the person renting the property, from police or else the authority concerned and that will be called as access.
5. **Next comes the Commercial Appropriation:** Commercial appropriation is also known as misappropriation, that involves an unauthorized use of an individual's organization's prominence in order to benefit someone else. If the public figure is officially participating in an event being covered, he or she can be considered a part of the event. In such cases the camera shots may dwell on the person as much as they wish.
6. **Another legal issue is Defamation:** Defamation is defined as the communication to a third party of false and injurious ideas to tend to lower the community's estimation of the person, expose the person to contempt or ridicule, or injure them in their personal, professional, or financial dealings. Libel is defamation by written or printed word and is generally considered more serious than slander, which is defamation by spoken words or gestures also.

It should be obvious that reporters and producers must carefully check any questionable material before broadcast or distribution. At one TV station the executive producer, the news director, and the states atomies view questionable segments.

The Media Policies - Laws for Electronic Journalism, we will deal now are nothing but for the broadcast media was under complete monopoly of the Government of India. The Supreme Court clearly differed from the monopolistic approach and emphasized that, every citizen has a right to telecast and broadcast to the viewers/listeners any important event through electronic media, television or radio and also provided the Government had no monopoly over such electronic media as such monopolistic power of the Government was not mentioned anywhere in the Constitution or in any other law prevailing in the country.

This judgment, thus, brought about a great change in the position prevailing in the broadcast media, and such sector became open to the citizens.

Let us learn about different types of laws that are present in India.

The first and foremost is Broadcasting Code: This code is adopted by the Fourth Asian Broadcasting Conference in 1962 listing certain cardinal principles to be followed by the electronic media, and this is of prime importance so far as laws governing broadcast medium are concerned.

Although, the Broadcast Code was chiefly set up to govern the All India Radio, the following cardinal principles have ideally been practiced by all Broadcasting and Television Organization. Let me list them forward to you:

- To ensure the objective presentation of news and fair and unbiased comment
- To promote the advancement of education and culture
- To raise and maintain high standards of decency and decorum in all programmes

- To provide programmes for the young which, by variety and content, will inculcate
- To promote communal harmony, religious tolerance and international understanding
- To treat controversial public issues in an impartial and dispassionate manner
- To respect Human Rights and dignity
- To respect human rights and dignity

The next law is Prasar Bharati Act, 1990: The primary duty of the Act is to organise and conduct public broadcasting services to inform, educate and entertain the public and to ensure a balanced development of broadcasting on radio and television in the country.

The next act is Cable Television Networks Regulation Act, 1995: This act regulates the operation of Cable Television in the territory of India and regulates the subscription rates and the total number of total subscribers receiving programmes are transmitted in the basic tier.

Next regulation is Cable Television Network Regulation Amendment Bill, 2002: The Central Government may make it obligatory for every cable operator to transmit or retransmit programme of any pay channel through an addressable system as and when the Central Government so notifies. Such notification may also specify the number of free to air channels to be included in the package of channels forming the basic service tier.

Next act is the Copyright Act, 1957: According to this Act, 'copyright' means the exclusive right to commercially exploit the original literary, dramatic, artistic, musical work, sound recordings or cinematographic films as per the wishes of the owner of copyright subject to the restrictions imposed in the Act.

Although this Act, is applicable to all the branches of media, in some areas it is specific to this particular genre. In case of a Cinematographed film, to do or to authorise the doing of any of the following acts would lead to the infringement of copyright. Those acts are namely: -

- To make a copy of the film
- To cause the film, in so far, as it consists of visual images, to be seen in public and in so far as it consists of sounds to be heard in public
- To make any record embodying the recording in any part of the soundtrack associated with the film by utilizing such sound track
- To communicate the film by radio-diffusion

The Act also makes it cognizable offence for anyone to sell, hire, distribute, exhibit, possess or view any unauthorised recordings and prescribes severe penalties, including imprisonment, fines as well as confiscation of the equipment used for the purpose of such recording and exhibition. The Amendments to the Copyright Act also prohibit unauthorized transmission of films on the cable television.

In this age of media explosion, one cannot simply remain confined to the boundaries of the traditional media. The media world has expanded its dimensions by encompassing within its orbit, the widening vistas of cyber media etc. As a consequence, the laws governing them are also numerous. It is not within the scope of the laws to deal with the whole subject of media laws, the various branches of Media Communication, only makes aware of a journalist rights and facilitating him to exercise them within the framework of law existing in India and in the end furthering the cause of *"Freedom Of Speech And Expression"* and *"Dissemination of Knowledge"*.

Role, advantages and disadvantages of Electronic media

Coming to the Advantages of Electronic Communication. It requires only few seconds to communicate through Electronic media because of its quick transmission and the world has become a global village and the communication around the globe requires a second only. Today that is possible through electronic communication. Electronic communication saves time and money. For example, you can just text an SMS that is cheaper than a traditional letter or Electronic communication allows instant exchange of feedback. So, the communication becomes perfect using electronic media. And the feedback also is also very much easy.

Due to advancement of electronic media, one can easily control operation across the globe. Video and teleconferencing e-mail and mobile communication are helping managers in this regard. They can be easily accessed anywhere with a computer, if not atleast a smart phone or an IPod of just on your doorstep. They are also eco friendly and there is no need for wasting a paper.

Regarding the disadvantages of Electronic Communication:

The volume of telecommunication information is increasing in such a fast rate that business people are unable to absorb it within relevant time limit. It requires huge investment also for infrastructural development and Frequent change in technology also demands for further investment. Data or information, if faxed, may be distorted are so compared to the information through print media it has zero value in the eye of law. Data may not be retrieved due to system error or fault with the technology also may become a problem in undelivered data also. Hence, required service will be delayed. There is also the Technology that is changing everyday and therefore poor countries face problem as they cannot afford new or advanced technology. Therefore, poor countries need to be dependent towards developed countries for sharing global network.

CHAPTER XIV

SOFTWARE IN ELECTRONIC MEDIA (Radio)

History and Growth of radio in India

As food, clothing and shelter are part of our lives, so is the radio today. Slowly and silently, the radio has crept into our lives and is here to stay.

In India, as early as August 1921, The Times of India in collaboration with the post and Telegraph Department broadcasted a Special programme from its Bombay office. This was at the request of Sir George Llyod, Governor who listened to the programme of Pune. The first radio programme in India was broadcasted by the Radio club of Bombay in June 1923, it was followed by the setting up of a broadcasting service that began broadcasting in India in June 1927 on an experimental basis at Bombay and Calcutta simultaneously under agreement between Government of India and a private company called the Indian Broadcasting Company Limited, the programmes were going on. After that the development of broadcasting in India proceeded with many ups and downs and in climate of much uncertainty. Improvements in technology also supported change. The transistor was invented during "World War II". In 1930, the Indian Broadcasting Company handed over Bombay station to the Government and it was renamed as Indian State Broadcasting service (ISBS). It was renamed as All India Radio on 8th June, 1936. When India became independent, the All India Radio network had only six stations located at Delhi, Bombay, Calcutta, Madras, Lucknow and Thiruchirapalli with a total complement of 18 transmitters.

With the implementation of Prasar Bharti bill, All India Radio is operating independently having different nature of control by the government. Before 1976, television constituted as a part of All India Radio. After that, it was

separated from AIR and constituted into a new body and under a new banner Doordarshan. Now All India Radio is also called in the name of Akashvani like television that is called Doordarshan.

Then All India Radio began operating in 1936, as a government organization, with clear objectives to inform, educate and entertain the masses. All India Radio is a national service planned, developed and operated by the Ministry of Information and Broadcasting under the Government of India. After the independence, All India Radio had a network of six stations, complimentary

18 transmitters and covered only 2.5% of the area and 11% of the population. Today, AIR has a network of 215 broadcasting centres with 144 medium frequency, i.e. MW, 54 high frequency, i.e. SW and 139 FM transmitters. At present, there are 215 broadcasting centers, including 77 Radio Stations with 100% coverage.

Coming to the achievements of All India Radio, AIR has been broadcasting its programmes in Analogue Mode.

Short Wave achievement, i.e. SW: The Short Wave radio provides large coverage generally 1.6–30 MHz, but the reception quality is not satisfactory due to inherent sky wave propagation impairments.

Another achievement is Medium Wave, i.e. MW: In Medium Wave the coverage is limited due to conductivity considerations and the quality of reception is fairly better over SW

Another achievement is Frequency Modulation bands, this is also called FM Radio and though it provides excellent reception quality, the coverage is limited to Line of Sight only (LOS). So the All India Radio has embarked in the era of digital radio broadcasting on 16th January, 2009 by launching its first digital radio transmission in Short Wave Band by using

DRM Technology to bring significant improvement in the reception and coverage. DRM technologies enable content publishers to enforce their own access policies on content, such as restrictions on copying and viewing.

Now let us see the features of Radio and All India Radio Services. AIR has a three-tier system of broadcasting through which it caters to the information, education, and entertainment needs of the people. Those are:

1. **National Service:** The National channel of AIR started functioning on May 18, 1988. It covers nearly 76% of the population and 64% of the area of the country. It provides a judicious blend of information and entertainment to programmes, including news, high quality Hindustani, Karnatak and western music; investigative reports and features, magazines, plays, sports, and also Vividh Bharati, a causerie of people, men and matters of music and different regional matters.
2. **The next service is Regional Services:** The regional services cater to major linguistic and cultural groups. This service is offered by each State and Union Territory to the groups living in these areas. Except for news and national programmes of folks and music which are relayed from Delhi, the other programmes of each regional station directed at different groups such as farmers, workers, their children, women, and youth are produced at the regional stations and even the centres. The national service programmes are broadcast over short wave transmitter, which makes it possible for regional centres to relay them also.
3. **Another service is External Services:** The external services of All India Radio act as a bridge between India and outside world. The External Services Division (ESD) broadcasts programmes for 69 hrs per week every day in 24 languages- General overseas service in English, 15 other foreign languages and in 8 Indian languages for our listeners in different parts of the globe. External broadcasts project the Indian point of view of world affairs and acquaint the overseas listeners with the developments in India along with the information on the Indian life, and also the culture, tradition and heritage. It also broadcasts in Indian languages for Indian people settled abroad.

The programmes generally comprise news bulletins, newsreels, and current affairs, review of the India press, sports, and folk music and so on.

4. **There is one more service, i.e. Vividh Bharati:** The Vividh Bharati was started on 2nd October 1957, as a service of 'light entertainment' to compete with Radio Ceylon, which had begun directing a commercial service to India on powerful short wave transmitters. At present, there are 30 Vividh Bharati and commercial Broadcasting stations in the country. Sixty per cent of the time of the stations is devoted to film music and the rest is earmarked for devotional music, light music and spoken word programmes in the form of short plays, talk interviews, or talks etc. Sponsorships are also accepted for these programmes. Vividh Bharati service increased the popularity of radio as a mass communication medium. At present, this service is on the air for 12 hours and 45 minutes every day with an extra hour and a quarter on Sundays and holidays.
5. There is also News Services Division that produces 89 bulletins in 19 languages, which emanate from Delhi and are relayed by several other All India Radio stations. In addition to these bulletins, the Regional News Units, 41 in all, located in different parts of the country, produce as many as 134 regional and 7 external news bulletins. The News Service division produces bulletins for listeners abroad in 24 languages.

There are also other Services through Radio to the audience:

Frequency Modulation is one of them and this broadcast is through the radio signals from transmitting station travel into the space without any hindrance. There is no reflection of signals by the upper atmosphere. It is just sufficient that the reception set is within the area of the station. It is often called FM radio station. Some stations are referred to as clear channel stations, which refer to powerful station broadcasting to wide area without any interference. It is essentially a local channel with a reach of 70 km radius from the place of transmission. Owing to its crystal clear reception it has traditionally been used for broadcasting music, often intercepted with local news and weather forecasts. FM was introduced in 1977 but it was not really activated. It was activated in 1992. All Metros like Delhi, Bombay, Calcutta and Madras etc. have a 24 hours FM service. FM has chatty, interactive style of programming and this radio substitutes as a friend.

There is also Phone-in-Programme: This provides simultaneous communication. People telephone to the broadcasting station on a given telephone number at the time of broadcast and ask questions and the experts at the station reply to their queries immediately.

Voice-Mail is also one of the service facility where people can telephone and record their requests, complaints, suggestions and also their appreciation and these messages are later retrieved and played back in a special voice Mail Programme with suitable replies to their queries.

There is also Radio Bridge: This is programme on special occasions and is broadcast live by up linking all the Radio stations through satellite. It represents a live interaction among the participants including listeners in different parts of the country. Presently 20 All India Radio stations have up linking facility.

There is also Radio Paging: A major application of the additional data service injected in the FM broadcast channel known as RDS and this is also radio paging. It would provide alert signals, emergency calls, valuable information etc., the service will be highly useful for medical professionals, business executives, commercial applications and emergency services. All India Radio has FM transmitters at 17 centres for this service.

Formats of Radio programmes

Now let us know about the formats of Radio Programmes. There are **three main pillars** of Radio programmes' composition, they are:

1. News
2. Music programmes
3. Spoken word programmes.

News programmes constituted 22.49% of the total radio programme composition. Music programmes include classical, folk, light, devotional, film and western music programmes. Talks, discussions, interviews are regularly arranged to provide a forum for all shades of opinion on outstanding national and international issues also. Radio drama figures both in All India Radio's general programmes as well as in the programmes for specific groups. Radio features and documentaries are the formats, which use the entire range of audio formats in a single programme, e.g. like narration, music, drama, interviews, poetry, sound effects, etc.

The Rural programmes are broadcasted from almost all, All India Radio stations in different languages and also in local dialects to provide educational and informational support to agriculture and rural development programmes. As an advertising medium also, it proved cheaper in reaching many of a time.

The radio programmes have also been relatively dependent of the pre and post broadcast activities of learners which can be like

- Features
- Discussions
- News Bulletins
- Drama and
- Talks

Let's start by exploring formats, what they are and a little about their structures also. A Good radio involves more than simply telling stories or expressing opinions. One of the major challenges is choosing the appropriate format for the issue you are covering and the audience you are trying to reach.

The Features: A feature is a report or story about a specific theme, issue, community or person. It is often a regular item in news or magazine show and a more inner discussion of a topic. Radio terminology can differ from station to station, so you may find that this type of report is also called a package.

There are also Discussions, which are just conversation between two or more people on a specific topic. On a radio program, discussions include a program between the host and guests or experts on the topic being discussed. Listeners may also be involved in the discussion if the program has a call-in portion for questions and comments.

There are also News Bulletins, which are the round-up of the main stories of the moment. Main stories, News bulletins usually appear at the top of the hour and shorter bulletins are often placed on the half an hour. They may also be integrated into news programs.

Drama: Dramas are fictional stories, but they are based on real-life events or situations. Drama is an effective tool to help listeners connect with issues on an emotional level. Radio dramas are widely used in Africa, Asia and Latin America, especially to present information about social issues.

A talk, this is not to be confused with a talk show, a style of radio program that will be reviewed later in this module and it is a short scripted story or commentary usually presented by the writer and based on personal experience, observation or analysis. It is often a personal account of the impact of an issue or an event in someone's life. It may also be an opinion statement about a political, ethical or moral issue. Talks can be used to highlight the impact of an issue on individuals or spark discussion on a topic. Generally, they are about two minutes long.

News Programs: A news program, sometimes also called a current affairs show is a compilation of features, reports, interviews and discussions about current events, developments and controversial issues.

There are also Magazine programs which cover Lifestyle, Health, Topical issues - from a human interest angle, rather than a hard news angle, and also about Travel, Youth, Gender issues. These programs can cover almost anything. Some magazine programs only cover one topic while others may cover small or several programmes.

There are also Talk Show Formats: In addition to using of discussions, there are also talk shows these are also being used in other formats to grab listeners' attention or to help them connect with the issue. Like for example: Drama, Talks using a combination of these formats, it will create a more diverse program and this drama can be used to introduce an issue for discussion and talks that could be used to add personal perspective to the topic

Script writing for Radio

Now let us deal with the Script writing for Radio. Script writing probably as many methods of writing as there are writers. It differs in very diversed way. Each author has his own process for developing and writing a script. So much is involved in writing a good script that it would be impossible to write it down in a page or two. If you have never written a script, here is a brief description of one process. If you are an old hand at writing scripts, use what works for you.

Let us see how to Write a Radio Script

Learning how to write a radio script is critical for proper execution of a radio performance. The script must include various cues for dialogue, music, and sound effects and be able to quickly and clearly communicate the writer's objectives to the cast and crew.

Here are different steps on how to write a radio script;

Step1:

Formulate a story idea. In that story idea, you have to outline your characters, write about the setting and also what is the conflict and finally the resolution.

Step2:

You have to write the narrative of the story. You have to put the "meat" of the story on the bones of your outline. Always keep the limitations of radio in your mind. You are writing for listeners, not viewers.

Step3:

You have to divide the narrative into scenes, with good descriptions of setting, character, and sound effects.

Step4:

Write the dialogue based on your narrative. Let your characters and sound effects give the listener a picture of the action in their mind.

Step5:

Put the story into radio script format. This includes:

a. **Write a page heading.** This is used to specify what program or episode you are working on and what page you are on in the script. It should be placed across the top of the page.

b. Next thing is you have to **Write a scene heading.** This specifies the scene number, description of the scene's location, and time of day.

c. You also have to **Include script cues.** There are three things a listener mainly retains from a radio drama: dialogue, music, and sound effects. Each of these audio elements or components are identified as a "cue"—because they happen at a given time in the script and the director may also instruct someone or "cue them" to produce it.

d. Then you have to **insert music cues.** Varying emotions can be achieved through the choice of music. So, clearly written instructions regarding music cues will greatly assist the cast and crew in influencing the mood of a given scene.

e. Now we have to include **the dialogue cues**. This helps the director and the actors prepare themselves for proper timing and execution.

f. Now **inserting the sound effect cues** helps to establish the scene or depict action. Sound effect cues are always underlined.

g. Now you have to **Compose your production notes.** Engineers cast or crew requires specific instructions that are handled as production notes--comments from the writer on how to coordinate cues or achieve particular effects. These need to be clear and precise.

<u>Step6:</u>

Edit your radio script after letting it sit for a few hours or days. A fresh set of eyes will help you catch any mistakes in grammar or plot. Consider having a third-party scrutinize the script for you.

<u>Step7:</u>

Present the script to your producer or editor and make revisions as necessary.

The effectiveness of a radio broadcast increases when the program writers take into account, vocabulary of the target group) and if organizers encourage listeners to participate in a post broadcast session, particularly if the broadcasts themselves are so designed as to draw the listeners to a participatory programme in the form of filling in checklists and other academic exercises". It also included programmes such as talk shows, weather reports, music, news summaries and many other entertainment programs. Thus, in its various formats radio is strongly striving to survive a challenge of television today.

CHAPTER XV

CINEMA AND FILM MEDIA

India is leader in film production. Indian cinema has yielded 28,000 feature films and thousands of documentaries so far. **The first exposing of celluloid in camera** by an Indian and its consequent screening took place in 1899, when Harish Chandra Bhatwadekar popularly known as Save Dada, shot two short films and exhibited them under Edison's projecting Kinetoscope.

Govind Phalke, more generally known as Dada Saheb Phalke and also the father of Indian cinema was responsible for the production of India's first fully indigenous silent feature film "Raja Harish Chandra" which heralded the birth of the Indian Film industry. The film had titles in Hindi and English and was released on May 3, 1913 at the coronation cinema in Bombay. In 1917, Bengal saw the birth of its first feature film. In Madras the first feature film' of South India 'Keechaka Vadham' was made by Nataraja Mudaliar in 1919. After stepping into 1920, the Indian cinema, gradually assumed the shape of a regular industry. The industry also came within the purview of the law.

The first Indian talkie "Alam Ara" produced by the Imperial film company and directed by Ardeshir Irani - released on March 14, 1931 at Majestic cinema in Bombay. The talkie had brought revolutionary changes in the whole set up of the industries. **The first International Film Festival of India** was held in early 1952 at Bombay and had a great impact on Indian Cinema. **The big turning point** came in 1955 with the release of Satyajit Ray and his classic 'Pather Panchali'. In Hindi cinema too, the impact of neo-realism was evident in some distinguished films like Bimal Roy's 'Do Bigha Zameen, 'Devdas', 'Madhumati', Raj Kapoor's 'Boot Polish', 'Shri 420' and 'Jagte Raho', Mehboob's 'Mother India' and so on.

In 1953, **the first color feature**, Jhansi Ki Rani was made. Mother India in 1957, Ganga Jamuna in 1961, Sangam (1964),

Bobby (1973), Sholay (1975), have been some of the successful films at the box office and trend setters in the commercial cinema. In sixties, mediocre films were made mostly to please the distributors and to some extent, meet the demands of the box office, such as, Mughal-E-Azam, Guide, Sahib Bibi Aur Gulam, Aradhana, etc. Satyajit Ray, Ritwik Ghatak and Mrinal Sen were the founder fathers of the new cinema in India. Roy was fortunate enough to present his films in almost all the leading film festivals of the world. The national and international awards won by Roy are numerous.

In seventies, **the trend for new wave cinema** started in India with the release of Mrinal Sen's "Bhuvan Shome" in 1969. This boosted the production of small budget films with simple plots but rich in resonance. It was followed by Sara Akash, Rajnigandha, Chhoti Si Baat, Chitchor, Swami, Arth. The new wave cinema movement continued with full spirit in seventies and eighties also. Some of the good movies like Manthan; Bhoomika, Junoon, 36-Chowringhee Lane, Mirch Masala, Trishagni were produced during this period. Nineties saw the revival of the musical love stories in Hindi cinema such as Qayamat Se Qayamat Tak, Chandni, Hum Aapke Hai Kaun, etc. so on and so forth.

In 20th century, Indian cinema, along with the Hollywood and Chinese film industries, became a global enterprise. Enhanced technology paved the way for upgrading from established cinematic norms of delivering product, altering the manner in which content reached to the target audience. Visual effects based, super hero science fiction, the epic films like Baahubali, Enthiran, and Ra.One have emerged as blockbusters. And also Indian cinema found markets in over 90 countries where films from India are screened.

Purpose and types of films

Coming to the purpose and types of films, Film is a story or event recorded by a camera as a set of moving images and shown in a cinema or on television. 'Cinema' and 'films' are used interchangeably but there is a difference between these two terms. Cinema is a theatre where films are shown for public entertainment.

Cinema has specific means to create imaginary time and space, and utilization of these means defines how cinematic a film is in a theatre where films are shown for the public entertainment. Films mean the particular movies that we see with all the elements they contain and cinema means the sum of the means made possible only by film technology, which distinguish cinema from the other arts. The term 'movies' is also used for the films when attempt is to provide enjoyment and relaxation.

Regarding the types of **cinema,** when we the talk, there are two major forms:

Commercial cinema –

- It primarily aims at providing entertainment to the people.
- It mostly resorts to fantasy to provide entertainment to people.
- For example: Films like Vaqt, Sholay, Muqhddar Ka Sikkandar, Hum Apke Hain Kaun, are a few examples.

Coming to the next one, Art cinema –

- It is with more realistic and relevant to the needs of the people and society.
- It is called 'parallel cinema' 'alternative cinema' or 'New wave cinema'.
- These new trend films are made at low cost, outside the main stream of commercial cinema.
- National Films Development Corporation provided institutional aid for the production of these films.
- Satyajit Ray, Shyam Benegal, Mrinal Sen, are some of the known art cinema proponents. However, many times this cinema faced difficulties in getting financier, or distributor. Many of them remain at award winning level only and never reach the masses due to these difficulties. With the popularity of television, some of the such films are telecast on television also. For examples, Chakra, Ankur, Nishant, Ardha Satya, Damul, Paar, Hazar Chaurashi Ki Maa etc.

Nowadays cinemas are broadly classified into **four major types** also:

1. First and foremost is Feature films:

   - Feature film means fictionalized film exceeding 2000 metres in length in 35 mm or corresponding length in other gauge or on video.
   - Feature film means a full length cinematograph film produced wholly or partly in India with a format and a story woven around a number of characters where the plot is revealed mainly through dialogue and not only through narration, animation, or cartoon depiction and does not include an advertisement in the film.
   - They are about a story enacted by a popular cast and usually has an ending.
   - These are produced for mass information and entertainment.
   - These films have the elements like comedy, drama, suspense, science fiction, detective, and horror elements.
   - They create cultural waves and to certain degree, change the attitude of the viewers also and increase information and modifying the behavior of the public.
   - The main objective of these films is not so much to convey a moral but firstly to entertain the audience. They continue to be most popular form of entertainment.

2. The next types of films are Documentary cinema:

   - Documentary is nothing but the dramatization of an idea or theme and
   - It uses the factual material in order to dramatize its idea, it tells its simple story in terms of human beings and human interests.
   - Sometimes it uses professional actors in some scenes.

- Of late, documentaries also have acquired a reputation for artistic merit.
- They last longer than feature films due to their informative and educative nature.

3. The next type is Sponsored cinema:

   - Many commercial organizations produce films as part of a broad advertising and public relations programme on their products, achievements and also approaches to their production etc.
   - This is to attract the consumer, financiers, and excellent professionals as well as to compete in fast advancing market system.

4. The next type is Educational cinema:

   - These films are produced with instructional objectives, for **example,** Films on details of geography or history, moon, atmosphere, non-formal education in slums, ideal schools or so on or so forth.
   - These films can be used as part of main lesson or supplementary information also.
   - Some of the documentaries also can be used as educational films.
   - In India educational films have not been used widely.

So let us see what the Advantages of Films are:

As a mass medium, they have similar advantages as television as far as motion and manipulation of time are concerned. Motion is essential for comprehending certain concepts and messages.

For example: Science experiments, operation of machines or industrial plants can be shown effectively with motion. Both the media show few hours long event in few minutes.

And the next advantage is the impact: The impact left by the films helps in shaping personal and social attitudes. They present the situation in a dramatic, recreation form, which brings reality also and assures the involvement of the viewer and leaves emotional impact.

Next advantage is it is a Versatile medium: It lends itself to instructional use in both large and small groups, and for individual study also. Technically, film allows a wider range of colors than video; furthermore, the actors vary more in terms of hue and portray a greater range of contrast then television. This holds viewers attention better than video or television.

Films provide for viewing of phenomena at extremely close range or from a vast distance, which is not possible in television and they can be used for variety of purposes such as entertainment and education, persuasion, changing motivation and opinions. The message conveyed through films are retained better due to its reality element. They allow for a creative production approach. It is possible to make different language and cultural versions of a film.

Coming to the Limitations, the main limitation of the films is its fixed pace. They move at a fixed pace and some viewers are likely to fall behind, if they are unable to keep pace with the pace of the film.

Next limitation is Dramatization, since films are mostly the dramatized presentation, they are chances of sophisticated treatment or exaggerated version of a situation or issue.

For example, if an adolescent has seen a film with generation gap theme, it is likely that he will take this melodrama in a literary sense and feel that he is also having to face many problems due to generation gap in his relationship with his parents and teachers.

Next limitations is regarding the limits, it is very difficult to define the limits of what is "controversial" in films. For example, the film "Aandhi" was banned during the emergency period in India. It was labeled as controversial film. When released, people did not find anything controversial or objectionable in the film. The commercial films are made with the audience's preference in mind, but there is hardly any feedback mechanism.

They are costly, and require huge amount of finances. They requires highly sophisticated equipment for production as well as projection. Each film requires individual distribution of network, which requires investment of large amount of money and time also.

Also requires trained personnel: Film production also requires trained personnel such as Director, Photographer, Sound effects expert, Musician, Editor, etc. once the film production is complete, it is very expensive to make any changes in the film.

Principles in writing for educational films

Let us see what are the principles in writing for an educational films. Films have been a popular mass medium. With the technological advancement in film and film production as a field has become very competitive and challenging also.

Film production or Filmmaking or in an academic context, it is usually called **film production** is the process of making a film involves a number of discrete changes including an initial story, idea, or commission, through scriptwriting, casting, shooting, sound recording and reproduction, editing, and screening the finished product before an audience that may result in a film release and exhibition also.

Film production offers mainly **five careers:**

- **The first and foremost is Cinematography:** This is a technical job which requires creativity and imagination to make a time with best photographic effects. Director explains the cinematographer about the type of shot he/she wants and then he has to work out the details of the types of shots, angles etc.
- **Next one is Film direction:** A **film director** controls a **film's** artistic and dramatic aspects, and visualizes the script while guiding the technical crew and actors in the fulfillment of that vision. Directors are responsible for the treatment of films. They have to know about every aspect of film production. They are required to guide actors and technicians so as to produce a film of vision.

- **Next one is very importantly the Sound Recording and Sound Engineering:** This is also a technical job, which is required to insert sound effects according to the mood and theme of the film.
- **Next one is Film Editing:** This involves assembling and cutting the finished film in order to create a film with proper sequencing and organization, which gives meaning to the film and highlights the theme. It is done with the help of editing machine in the editing room.
- **There is Art direction also** where other aspects, which include the direction of sets, choreography, costume designing etc. will be dealt and that also is a very important career.

There are **five major stages** in Film Production:

1. **Development** — The first stage in which the ideas for the film are created, rights to books/plays are bought etc., and the screenplay is written. Financing for the project has to be sought in this stage itself and greenlit.
2. Next one is **Pre-production**—Preparations are made for the shoot, in which cast and film crew are hired, locations are selected, and sets are built.
3. **Next stage is Production**—The raw elements for the film are recorded during the film shoot.
4. Next stage is **Post-production** where images, sound, and visual effects of the recorded film are edited.
5. The last stage is **Distribution**, where the finished film is distributed and screened in cinemas and released to home videos also.

A Short film is any film not long enough to be considered as a feature film. No consensus exists as to where the boundary is drawn but a short film is an original motion picture that has running time of 40 minutes or less including all credits.

So let us see the steps in making a short film:

The first and foremost is **Script:** Here it is crucial to remember that film is a Visual medium. You don't tell your audience your story, you show them. Writing what they will see and what they will HEAR is nothing but a Script. When it happens, it may be just done with a look, often improvised on the movie set. So Script should be written with the pictures, sounds, speeches, and leave the rest for the filmmakers.

The script format for documentaries and audio-visual presentations which consists largely of voice-over matched to still or moving pictures is different again and uses two-column format which can be particularly difficult to achieve in standard word processors, at least when it comes to editing or rewriting.

Many script-editing software programs include templates for documentary formats involving

- Focusing on story, dialogue,
- Formatting, character, plot,
- Theme, momentum and the
- Document

Next one is the **Support:** Emphasis should be given also to focus on the filmmaking team, i.e. the Producer, director, cast, crew, and their roles and responsibilities.

Coming to the **Storyboard aspect,** it is the graphic organizer in the form of illustrations or images displayed in sequence for the purpose of pre- visualizing a motion picture, animation, motion graphic or interactive media sequence. A film storyboard is essentially some section of the film produced beforehand to help film focusing on how to turn the script into a series of pictures and images able to be filmed.

Storyboards for films are created in a multiple step process. They can be created by hand drawing or digitally on a computer also.

The main characteristics of any storyboard are:

- Visualize the storytelling.
- Focus the story and the timing in several key frames, which are very important in animation and
- Define the technical parameters, i.e. the description of the motion, the camera, the lighting, etc.

Coming to the Steps in Storyboarding:

If drawing by hand, the first step is to create or download a storyboard template. These look much like a blank comic strip, with space for comments and dialogue. Then sketch a "thumbnail" storyboard. Some directors sketch thumbnails directly in the script margins. The common storyboard software for desktop are Articulate storyline, Twine, Celtx.

Coming to the Structure: Focusing on structuring and synchronizing all aspects of the film before it is shot, such as the design, locations, make-up, hair, catering and any specific requirements of the film are to be taken care of also in the structural aspect.

Next comes the **Shooting, i**n filmmaking and video production, **a shot is nothing but a series of frames that runs for an uninterrupted period of time.**

These film shots are an essential aspect of a movie where angles, transitions, and cuts are used to further express emotion, ideas and movement. This term "**shot**" can refer to two different parts of the filmmaking process focusing on the shoot itself and things to consider and be aware of.

Focusing on the post-production stage including the editing, music, sound effects and pickup shots is also required for the sake of shape.

Coming to the SCREEN, Focusing on putting your film in front of an audience and using it as a 'calling card' to get into the industry is also very important.

So finally, what **makes a good idea for a film?**

Firstly, drama is about a conflict, so 'good' ideas for short films are those that can sustain conflict throughout. The conflict might keep an audience interested for the length of a short film.

Films are about a central dramatic question. Central dramatic questions are always in terms of your main character and must last the entire film. As soon as the question is answered, the film is often over.

A good way to start is by choosing a subject you are interested in or an experience you have had.

Try the following steps to get you thinking:

- Write down your interests or passions, in any order.
- Group your interests together to find a pattern or link between them.
- Select the thing or subject you are most passionate about and consider something you want to express on that idea; for example, a thought, or a message or an opinion you want to convey to a reader or an audience.
- Write some possible thoughts for messages or opinions underneath the actual subject or area of interest, like that.

So I just put forth some examples about some ideas that to get you started:

- A holiday you've seen or you have been on, the message can be – there's no place like home
- A childhood memory, sometimes one must let go of the past to move on

Like this a screenplay or script is a blueprint for creating a motion image. It can be modified from a previous work.

For example—from a short story, play, novel or it could be from an original work in and of itself.

Most screenplays are anticipated to be written in 12 point font size, devoid of bolding or italicizing. This section depicts the elements used to develop a screenplay.

The Basic Script Formatting has three bodies of a script, i.e.

- The Headlines
- A Narrative
- Dialogues.

Each of these has three points to remember.

The Headlines contains Master Headlines which include camera location exterior (Ext) or Interior, inside (Int) and then Scene location, i.e. the Local Race Track, Time (Day or Night).

Then the **Secondary scene heading** will also be there. **"Special headings"** will be there for things such as montages i.e., the technique of selecting, editing, and piecing together separate sections of film to form a continuous whole with dream sequences, flashbacks, flash forwards, etc.

Here in this special headings you also will be having **Narrative Description** also, like

1. Action
2. Character and settings, such as visual settings and
3. Sounds

Coming to the Dialogue:

1. The name of the person speaking appears at the top, i.e. in CAPS.
2. The actors direction (parenthetical or wryly). Try to avoid these as much as possible.
3. Both the director and actor will appreciate it.
4. The speech.

The Steps in this dialogue is nothing but there will be a Title page:

a. Since a title page is the first indication to a producer that you are either professional or an amateur, so make sure that your screenplay is quite gripping type.

b. Title should be highlighted, either by underline or by quotation marks.
c. In the bottom of it, put contact information or any copyright information.

There will also be **Transitions,** these are short descriptions illustrating how the film will move from one scene to the next. The only time to employ transition is if it is vital to tell a story you can make use of it.

For example—

- You can use Time Cut to specify the passage of time.
- Dissolve to indicate that time has passed.
- You can make use of Match Cut if you want to demonstrate that there is some association between something we just view and something in the new scene.

There are **Scene headings** also which are also called slug lines, which mark out the commencement of a new scene in a screenplay. If the scene is exterior, it begins with "EXT" and if the scene takes place indoor, than "INT." When pursuing this descriptor, the name of the location of the scene should be materialized in caps. This is then followed by a space, a hyphen, another space, and then the time of day. Scene headings should have a margin of 1.5 inches from the left, 1 inch from the right.

And there should also be page breaks, when the paragraph of action or dialogue is split up across the pages, the break is supposed to come among the sentences and not previous to the second line of the paragraph.

Next comes the **Action,** it represents what can be observed on the screen and is always in the present tense

Then Dialogue in screenwriting, wherever or whenever a character verbalizes, it is nothing but a dialogue, even if it is a monologue also it should be mentioned.

CHAPTER XVI

SOFTWARE IN FOLK MEDIA

Historical perspective of folk media

Folk media are cultural resources that accumulate indigenous knowledge, experiences and expressions passed down from generation to generation.

Traditionally folk modes of communication are as old as man. It is indisputable fact that local or primitive communities had their traditional patterns of communication which were peculiar to their environment and situations. The desire to exchange message and share common ideas must have propelled our forefathers to introduce diverse media through which they could express different feelings and also communicate certain situations. The early man's first means of communication were system of distinct sounds or calls and each call signaled specific circumstances such as 'food and danger '.

These Folk modes of communication were in place long before the advent of modern means of communication. Gestures and drawing of pictures developed as secondary method of communication and gradually, introduced into languages and pictorial writings. As the traditional societies developed, better traditional methods of communication were invented. Starting with the simplest vocal and gestures, signals rooted in their physical structure, human beings developed a whole range of non-verbal means for conveying messages. Folk modes include music, dance, drums, oral messages signals, fire, drawings and other forms of graphic symbols like pictogram. These modes of communication have survived and are still in use. They are very relevant especially in rural areas, even in the era of high information technology. Further, it is asserted that traditional communication is made up of a great variety of socially accepted cultural practices, social organizations and patterns of speech and is also a product of many fields of endeavor such as music, linguistics, religion, history, sociology, mythology, the performing art just to mention a few.

Man's earnest desire to express feelings, messages, and share ideas motivated him to create various modes of communication through which he could communicate with his fellow being. By large, those folk media of communication were developed into coherent languages using specific signals, symbols and pictures to represent messages. Traditional patterns of communication have the same characteristics even though they vary from one community to another. These characteristics are generally oral mode, limited audience, impression, consumer friendly, no specialized training required, lack of fidelity, cheap, binds people together and non-alienating. The mass media have always being vested with the responsibilities of developing the people for effective participation. The folk media functions just same as the media which is to inform, educate and entertain but the only differences is that, it is restricted to only one area.

The folk media are the people media such as songs, riddles, dance, face to face, folktales, theatre performance, village square, festivals, town criers, talking drums, harvest, churches, mosques, etc. Traditional modes of communication unlike the mass media play greater roles in the development of the rural masses.

Traditional media means the mediums through which the cultural traits are passed from generation to generation. It is born and expressed in the idiom of people's culture and has always seemed to entertain, educate and propagate the existing ideas and attitudes. Keeping in view their intimacy with the people at the local levels, folk media channels prove to be powerful tools of communication in the rural society.

Traditional media are an effective and important part of the communication system. These are unique in nature, as they resemble the day-to-day life pattern of the rural masses. These media are a source of popular entertainment for the

rural audience, in addition to providing instruction and information. Our country has a rich heritage of folk arts, folk dance, folk tales, epics, ballads and plays that can be used for development work. The folk arts are popular media of conveying the message to the rural mass in the shortest time. These are used for moral, religious, socio, political and entertainment purposes. The folk media are close to the heart and minds of the people. Rapport is immediate and direct. Folk media are being enjoyed by persons of different age groups at a very low cost. They are flexible and easy to accommodate new themes.

Folk entertainments can provide fresh and interesting programme material for the mass media making them, more acceptable to both the rural and urban audiences. The folk media can be usefully employed to educate the non-school masses. In sum, the role of the traditional media in a country like ours is of paramount importance in enriching our culture and tradition as also disseminating information and educating our rural folk.

Characteristics and Types of traditional folk media

Characteristics of traditional folk media:

- Indigenous in nature. Generally rural in origin.
- Transmitted from generation to generation through oral means alone
- No source of confirming the authenticity of folk art.
- It has no grammar.
- Indicates and integrates the emotional behaviour of the practicing sector.
- Represents the practicing sector of region, religion, family or group that can be differentiated from the other
- Limited area of operation
- Becomes victim to the onslaught of modern foreign media occasionally.
- As long as the contents and formats satisfy psychological and social needs of people, they will be carried forward by people themselves. Hence, the traditional media communication can put fresh contents in folk media.

- Folk media will never die but continue in spite of several obstacles in modern age. Its utilization has its impact even across cultural religions with blended forms and modified contents
- Traditional folk media have their own specific language, rhythm, music, style and form
- It is very much cheap, easy and convincing comparatively than modern media

Different Types of Traditional Folk Media Puppetry

It is one of the important traditional media for communicating technology in the villages. Puppetry is believed to be the oldest form of popular theatre in India. The term, sutradhar (string holder) was used for the director or the stage manager in the live, classical (sanskrit) theatre of ancient India (AD 100-1000). Experts reason that this use of the terminology derived from the puppet theatre is an evidence that puppetry preceded the live theatre in India.

In ancient India, especially in the South, the puppeteers were respected as intellectuals. They were usually patronized by kings and wealthy families and enjoyed immense prestige. The art of puppetry was popular both as pure entertainment and as an educational medium.

It is an inexpensive activity. It is an easily acquired art and even crudely made puppets when played with a lively sense of drama can hold an audience. The puppet play can impart lessons on health, literacy, agriculture, home-making; education, employment, rural youth activities, recreation, etc.

There are many types of puppets:

- String puppets (originated in Rajasthan),
- Glove puppets (source unknown),

- Rod puppets (Orissa and Tamil Naidu) and
- Shadow puppets (Kerala and Orissa).

Puppets can make an impact, if properly used with the active participation of the local people. Local dialect should be used if at all a foreigner' wants to stage a performance in a village. Puppetry attracts all age-groups.

Drama

Drama is a theatrical performance around a theme by some people who have rehearsed for it. This is also a good source of communication, entertainment and education for the villagers. The effectiveness of folk drama varies from message to message. One-act plays depict the village life, its problems and solutions; can be written and prepared with simple themes. The messages communicated through the traditional media gain access to the mind through both ears and eyes and the mind produces a sense of richness of meaning in the individual. This creates a high degree of interest and makes learning more permanent.

The subjects for drama stories may be on less yieldsof crops and the role of demonstrations on improved practices, schemes of the rural development programmes, role of democratic decentralization through village leaders, youth, Mahila and Krishak mandals, how to handle village problems like child marriage, wastage of money through ceremonies, dowry, solving problems of education, health, sanitation, role of co-operatives and extension wing and how villagers can be benefited from it, etc. Drama can be arranged at a common place in the village where the maximum gathering can be held. The time of presentation should suit the convenience of almost all villagers. People feel happy if seeing, hearing and action go simultaneously during the performance.

Folk theatre forms:

Tamasha

Tamasha is an extremely lively and robust form of folk theatre, going back to over 400 years. In this form, some topic is selected and then a chorus of six to eight male singers cum performers and two or more female dancer-singers make the troupe. The more vigorous form of tamasha is called song troupes and is believed to be the genuine or real form. It has a cast of three to six female dancer singers (one of whom is the star artist) a tabla player and a harmonium and tundun player. The story part is the next element. The most important is the performance. The story of tamasha in the form of agricultural dialogue, song and dance is based on stories derived from myth and folklore. It is in this section that comments are made on contemporary and social problems. Government-sponsored tamasha troupes also educate the masses on family planning. Tamasha needs no elaborate act or costumes and place and time.

Nautanki

Nautanki is like other folk drama forms. It has a simple dramatic structure comprising small units led by a Ranga or Sutradhara- the narrator. Music is of prime importance in this folk drama. The main musical instruments used are kettle drum and dholak. As in opera, the dialogues are sung to popular folk melodies but now even to film tunes. The nautanki form is popular in the fields of agriculture and rural development. It can be in the form of Doha, Thumari, Dadra, Sher, Gazal and Quawwali which are very common among the rural people in many states. This dramatic form may easily be adopted in the social, agricultural and rural development programmes. The people can be educated through the medium to bring about desirable changes in their behaviour.

Keertana or Harikatha

This is a religious folk theatre. The Keertana or Harikatha is a kind of concentrated drama or monodrama in which a gifted actor enters a whole series of characters. Saint Narada is believed to have invented and practised the form with great success. It is believed to have spread from Maharashtra to Karnataka and Tamil Nadu about 150 years ago. It is a mainly associated with the Bhakti movements in religion and literature. It was used by saints like Kabir, Guru' Nanak, Farid and Tukaram to preach the faith as also to bring about social reform and political change. It is such a potent weapon in social education that

Lokmanya Tilak is reported to have said if he was not a journalist, he would have been a keertankar.

Harikatha is also used by Central and State governments to educate the masses on family planning, developmental activities, democratic values and national integration with help of Keertankar or Kathakars. All India Radio and the Doordarshan too are using the keertan form for broadcasts aimed at industrial workers and rural audiences.

Street play

In this form, one narrates a story which is related to a particular theme. These plays are not like theatre but they attract a large number of people. They also have some music built in by way of folk songs adopted to the theme. The only material used in this form is a number of banners on which slogans are written. It is a non-costume, no-property no--script play. It is also known as Nukad play. Street plays are increasingly used to spread messages of family planning, sanitation, adult education, etc and they create awareness against social evils.

Folk Music – Music passed on for the races of people from generation to generation.

Folk song

Any music composed on idioms is folk song. The villagers have a great fascination for their folk songs. We go closer to them if we participate with them and organize such functions during exhibitions, meetings, film shows, drama, etc. Songs connected with agriculture and rural development programmes and practices in local dialects can be composed and sung easily as they also provide entertainment. This is a good way of conveying information to the villagers. Song competitions can also be arranged.

They are a good source of attracting the people and as such help extension programmes indirectly. They are part of cultural programme. The monotony of discussion of serious nature in a meeting can be broken by light songs. The

song should be composed on the subjects which are to be communicated to the people. They should be in the form of a story with some moral. The tune of the song should be popular and local to which the villagers are accustomed to. It will always be preferred if the song has just one message to convey. A few words by way of explanation will be appreciated before singing is started. The song can be followed with a little more explanation of its theme. Seasoned singers are liked by everybody but new voices are also welcome.

Folk dance

During the harvesting season and festivals, folk dances are aroused in the villages as they are helpful in collecting the people. The youth present Bhangra during the harvesting period. The folk dances reveal not only the individual talents of the people but the collective traditions of all the countries, the characteristics of the community and a love for rhythm.

Folk dances are mainly grouped under three heads:

i. Community folk dances held on the main religious festivals, social occasions, Kisan Melas and other occasions when special agricultural activities are carried out;
ii. Folk dances' are also preserved by hereditary, professional families and groups who perform at birth, betrothal and marriage ceremonies in the villages; and
iii. Tribal dances rooted as they are expressive of their magical philosophies of life.

Story-telling

Story-telling has been one of the best and most commonly used methods of instruction in informal education, religious propagation, rural development, etc. Over the years, certain etiquettes have been developed that are associated with story-telling. Before the story teller begins the narration, he asks, Are you ready to listen? The listeners respond with 'Yes' sound. This ensures proper attention when the story is narrated. The listeners often make some kind of sound at regular intervals to express attention. So important topics which help in proper development of the rural people can be touched through the stories. **Riddles**

This is also an educational device through which elders used to communicate knowledge. Sometimes these riddles are very helpful in conveying the real meaning of technology. Some puzzles are given to the rural people who help them understand the use of proper practices in the crop cultivation, home- making, etc.

Proverbs

Proverbs which prevail in oral civilization represent the essence of rural wisdom and knowledge. They are the sound symbols of culture and have survived for centuries; their use is quite frequent in oral culture. Proverbs are very creative in knowing the importance of information or idea as they also tell the meaning of the real message.

Here are some examples for proverbs:

Blood is thicker than water – Family relationship is stronger than others. **If the blind lead the blind, both shall fall**- If a person lacking in some expertise leads others, all of them shall fail.**There's a black sheep in every family** – One member in every family doesn't fit into the characteristic of the family.

Bioscope

This is also a popular folk medium used for entertainment and for propagation of information on education, agriculture, etc. Bioscope consists of a box made of light wood. It contains quite a number of folding doors, each like a panel hinged on one side with another panel with colourful figures and mythological episodes and incarnations of gods and goddesses painted and filed as pictures with the narration of the story by the story teller. This is helpful in conveying the people about educational messages like vegetable preservation, mosquito control, cultivation of different crops, etc. This can be made interesting with musical narration. The narrator unfolds each door and conveys, the message to the audience accordingly.

Munadi (Announcements)

This medium is very old. In this form, the drum is beaten and the attention of the audience is arrested and then the message is delivered. This medium is normally used to inform the people about some happenings or other important extension activities. This is mostly preferred by the rural people as it is used for dissemination of information followed by drum beating.

Example: for giving message about meeting, demonstration, field-day or any other activity. Usually chowkidars of the village do this job.

Wall paintings

The use of this medium has possibly evolved from an age--old practice of drawing or writing on walls. They are silent unlike traditional theatre and if they use words, they make themselves meaningless also to the non-literate majority. Yet, they are near permanent. A speech or film comes to an end soon, but the wall paintings stay as long as the weather or the organization concerned allows them to last. Perhaps, the greatest advantage of the medium is the power of the picture completed with its local touch. The images used have strong emotional association with the surroundings, a feat impossible for even a "moving" visual medium like television which must use general images to cater to the greatest number of viewers. Illiteracy, of course, is no bar for the wall paintings, if the message is conveyed by the picture alone and the words are only an adjunct. Indian experience in wall paintings communication by the government can still activate its potential in rural areas.

The forms of folk media are many. Un-official estimate of folk media existing in India runs around 6000 in number. With a little variation, all these forms can be included into various groups such as – puppetry, drama, Harikatha (Story of God), story-telling, folklore, tales, ballad singing, pad recital (visual aid), kavad (story box),folkdance, folksongs, street play, riddles, proverbs etc. Different Types of Traditional Folk Media include puppetry, theatre forms, folk music, folk dances, drama, storytelling and riddles.

Advantages & limitations of traditional media and Threats ofmodern media on folk media The folk and traditional media have their routes in the tradition and experience of a large majority of the population and also that they have a reach much more extensive than any of the modern technological media. The folk media have certain clear-cut advantages.

Advantages of Folk media

Personal contact: The appeal of folk media is quite personal and at an intimate level because it has got direct influence on people.

Language Familiarity: As in the case of colloquial dialects the familiar format and content of mass media gives much clarity in communication. **Rapport building:** The different forms of mass media can be exploited to cater to the needs of the people for immediate and direct rapport.

Flexibility: The folk media is so flexible that new themes can be accommodated in them.

Combination: Indian folk forms are a mixture of dialogue, dance, song, humour, moralising and prayer.

Impact: Though the folk media attracts a small audience, the impact on them is at a much deeper level inviting the audience participation.

Entertainment: Moral instruction campaigned is with entertainment. **Self expression:** Being dramatic and lyrical, it satisfies our innate need for self expression.

Cultural Heritage: The tradition and culture of ancestors are preserved and disseminated by the folk media in a lively manner.

Limitations of traditional folk media

- Threat to traditional folk media is a regular with the development of film industry, radio, television and video, the Indian traditional media gradually disappearing.
- Focus of attention of planners on modern media.
- Scale of reach to masses is very less unlike as in case of technology based electronic media.
- Changes in social system such as urbanization and literacy rate leading to more individual listening or viewing rather people are preferring community listening or viewing
- Considering the traditional media as out dated and irrelevant by the present generation.

- Traditional folk media is functioning mostly as unorganized sector.
- Even to revive traditional folk forms identification and selection of good artists is very difficult.
- Lack of encouragement to talented artists in traditional media leading to decline of folk media.
- Lack of proper understanding of traditional media and its nature.
- Range of choice of forms is very low.

Threats to Traditional Folk Media:

The traditional folk media is fading away gradually if not, disappearing due to modern electronic media such as film industry, radio, television, video, computers etc.

Reasons:

- At present, the attention of planners is much focussed on modern media
- Direction of change from oral communication to technology based electronic media
- Change in social system such as urbanisation and increase in literacy rate
- Expanding sources of financial and Human resources
- Considering the traditional folk media as out dated and irrelevant by present generations
- Invasion of commercial organizations on consumer appetites through exaggerated advertisements
- Lack of encouragement to talented folk artists
- Lack of proper understanding of traditional folk media and its nature by the present generations

Selection and use of folk media in development

The traditional folk media will be taken to mean the vehicle through which messages are carried from one end (variously or specifically called source, speaker, writer, artist, musician, or dancer) to another (receiver, target, listener, reader, or viewer). Folk media will therefore refer to the vehicle the common people or rural folk employ for the delivery of their messages. Folk dance, folk music, folklore, should therefore of necessity be immense value as communication tools, collectively called folk media, to anyone involved in the dissemination of information to the rural community. For instance, when a child is born to a young mother there are customs that the mother must know. When women are pounding maize in mortars at home they sing songs that speak about various experiences from their world. When village elders come together to listen to complaints made by someone from the village, they use proverbs and riddles to express themselves. Sometimes they will even tell a folktale, which reinforces the point they want to make. In this way, wisdom is shared and passed on from generation to generation.

The communication potential of Indian traditional performing art has been proved time and again by many instances. *Alha*, the popular ballad of Uttar Pradesh and its counterparts, like *Laavani* of Maharashtra, *Gee- gee* of Karnataka, *Villupaattu* of Tamil Nadu, *Burrakatha* of Andhra Pradesh and *Kabigan* of Bengal which changed their content and focus depending on the contemporary need, were effective in arousing the conscience of the people against the colonial rule of the British.

Social Communication through Folk Media

Some sociologists, educationists, psychologists and anthropologists have described the process of communication through various models. Aristotle says that all these three elements, i.e., speaker, speech and audience are essential for communication. These can be organized to study the process through the person who speaks, the speech he produces and the person/audience who listens. Such communication takes place in a face-to-face manner in traditional folk media.

The stylised vocabulary of puppet theatre in India carries a relevant message of social awareness, historical and traditional identity and moral value system. It is used as a medium for politicising people and drawing them into popular organisations and struggles. Puppet theatre is fully integrated in the ritual observances and the social milieu of the rural people in India. Puppet theatre has shown remarkable staying power against all kinds of vices. It is also used as a means of protest against oppression and a means of stirring up people's anger to action.

The Ramalila of Ramnagar is one such important theatrical genre which provides an opportunity for the young and old, rich and poor to come together for 16 to 20 days preceding the Dussehra to witness this vast display of human life. Each section of the city constructs raised platforms or transforms streets or terraces or gardens as the case may be, into palaces, woods and streams. The whole city is the stage, the arena of the performance. The play moves in succession day after day and the audience move with it form setting to setting.

Role of folk media in developmental Communication

Many development planners in the Third World now appreciate the use of folk media as a mode of communication to explain development programmes. This may be because of the ineffectiveness of the mass media in reaching those at whom the messages are targeted. Therefore, decision makers have started to take a second look at the use of folk media to generate local participation in development projects. UNESCO discussions focused specially on the potentiality of the various forms of traditional media and the technique of their production as well as integration with the mass media for motivational purposes. The United Nations Environmental Programme (UNEP) must be cited for taking interest in folk media to carry across to various audiences, the UNEP message of the need for a better environment for mankind.

In India, peasants, agricultural labourers, women, tribals, bonded labourers and other oppressed groups are rediscovering the potential of traditional arts and media as a weapon in their struggle for land, water, forest better working and living conditions, human rights. Folk arts are used for peace education and conflict resolution on a wide scale in India. Increasing number of people are turning to theatre by the people for the people and of the people as a means of mobilizing people for action for achieving social justice, peace and harmony.

The Task of Communication Expert

The communication expert must learn to manipulate folk media to achieve maximum impact through symbols and a system with which the rural community is already familiar. Once that level of understanding has been achieved, the villagers themselves will participate in devising the most effective medium from a wide range of folk media. Communication experts must understand these by working with the rural community. In that way, when they come to modernize or nationalize the message for purposes of dissemination nation-wide, they will concentrate on using symbols and images that make sense to the folk in the villages. Local trees, animals, landscape and weather will begin to play a major part in the way messages are echoed and delivered.

A Method for Efficient Communication

Now we shall take a brief look at a proposed method for increasing the efficiency of communication strategy for better results. They are **multi- media approach, package plan, utilising rural structures and village functionaries, and objective evaluation of the strategy.**

For an enhanced communication, the support of mass media channels would be necessary. The multi-media approach holds glamour for the field, covers different aspects of the message and interacts with different sections of people simultaneously. Together with folk media documentary films, printed material, phased broadcasts and telecasts, mutually support each other in the cause of effective motivational communication strategy. Its benefits are multiple for each medium makes up for the deficiency of the other, and all together make communication proficient and productive.

The second suggestion is of the package plan. The package plan is an integrated time bound work programme. It eliminates time lags between communication, extension and service. It brings to completion the efforts of the communicator. Time lags between communication and extension, and extension and service are often responsible for the failure of a goal- set communication strategy. Hence, the gaps as far as possible should be eliminated.

The third suggestion is to utilise the rural structures and village functionaries. Motivation for action could be energised by change-agents who are inter-personal communicators. It is very advantageous to look for such change-agents in the rural situation itself. It is necessary to identify the motivators in village teachers, priests, elders etc. For example, the village postman is a potential change-agent when motivated and harnessed for development. The service of the traditional folk artists will draw good result with such village-based functionaries.

The fourth or the last suggestion is to have an objective evaluation of the strategy. It is very useful to collect the information from local observers, experienced informants and the artists themselves. The feedback received helps us to see whether there is any need for change. The general assessment will not make any difference. So there is a need for evaluation of the quality and impact of the traditional folk media on the people. The efforts made will enhance the effect on the people.

The traditional media, however, are close to the hearts and minds of the people. They are more personal and intimate. Different folk media can be used to cater to different regions. Every village has its relevant music, dance or theatre. These traditional media can be used to reach these people in the process of change and development of the country. Traditional media uses a subtle form of persuasion by presenting the required message in locally popular artistic forms. This cannot be equalled by any other means of communication. So, if we want to inject the message of development among the rural masses we have to use the folk forms of this country in a more planned manner.

It is necessary to work towards giving more importance to our traditions and culture by communicating through folk art forms, which are more credible and have personal appeal to the daily lives of the people. Therefore folk media can efficiently be used even in the modern world. If we use folk media, in the coming days it will take more importance and used by more number of people.

Printed by Libri Plureos GmbH in Hamburg,
Germany